Brownie Points

D0565548

Brownie Points

over 100 outrageously delicious and easy recipes
based on america's favorite dessert

Lisa Slater

whitecap

Copyright © 2005 by Lisa Slater
Whitecap Books

All rights reserved. No part of this publication may be
reproduced, stored in a retrieval system, or transmitted
in any form or by any means, electronic, mechanical,
photocopying, recording or otherwise, without prior written
permission of the publisher. All recommendations are
made without guarantee on the part of the author or
Whitecap Books Ltd. The author and publisher disclaim
any liability in connection with the use of this information.
For additional information, please contact Whitecap Books,
351 Lynn Avenue, North Vancouver, British Columbia,
Canada V7J 2C4.

Edited by Elaine Jones
Proofread by Marial Shea
Design by Jen Eby
Photography by Christopher Freeland

Printed and bound in Canada

Library and Archives Canada Cataloguing in Publication
Slater, Lisa
    Brownie points : over 100 outrageously delicious and
easy recipes based on America's favorite dessert / Lisa Slater.

ISBN 1-55285-522-8
    1. Brownies (Cookery) I. Title.
TX771.S53 2004   641.8'654   C2004-904590-3

The publisher acknowledges the financial support of the
Government of Canada through the Book Publishing
Industry Development Program for our publishing activities.

Contents

THIS BOOK IS DEDICATED TO:

My parents, who are living proof that brownies promote longevity; my husband, Howard, who is living proof that brownies aren't fattening; and to my children, Jo and Ali, who are living proof that brownies make you smart.

To all of you: thank you for your loving support throughout the creation of Brownie Points.

ACKNOWLEDGMENTS AND APPRECIATIONS

This would have been a solitary project if not for all the enthusiastic testers who fearlessly sampled every brownie recipe. These include my colleagues at Whole Foods Market Toronto, as well as my husband Howard's many students and teaching associates. Thank you all for sacrificing your waistlines in pursuit of the perfect brownie recipe.

And then there are the many people at Whitecap Books, notably Alison Maclean, who encouraged the project from the beginning. Editing a cookbook may seem like a dream job—all those recipes to try before anyone else. In fact, it has to be one of the most painstaking forms of editing there is. Luckily, three people have pored over this manuscript: Alison Maclean, who whipped the project up and acted as an assistant to the photographer to create crisp, edgy photographs; Elaine Jones, whom I only know thanks to the miracles of email; and Marial Shea who pulled it all together, keeping me calm when I thought the whole project would melt like an underbaked brownie. The designer, Jen Eby, also went above and beyond the call of duty. To all of you, many, many thanks. I couldn't have done it without you and I look forward to working with you again.

And then there are a few family members who committed their time and attention to various parts of this book: my sister-in-law, Brenda, whose comments were both funny and perceptive, as well as my niece, Emma, who spent precious vacation days editing the final edition. Ladies, thank you, too.

Last but not least, are all the other members of my family, Abby, Morry, Maya, Ken, Simon, Eli, Michael, Kathy, Alexis, Nathaniel and Aaron, all of whom at one time or another encouraged the writing of these recipes through their enthusiastic consumption of my various brownie fantasies. Unbeknownst to them, they were all part of a covert experiment to see if anyone, at any time, would turn down chocolate desserts. Despite diets and dietary restrictions that ran the gamut from kosher to cholesterol, from low carb to low fat, the results are in and not all that surprising: no one can resist a chocolate dessert, especially if it's a brownie.

Introduction

the evolution of brownie points

BROWNIES ARE WHAT I CALL THE LITTLE BLACK DRESS of the baking trade: as perfect in a pan at the school fundraising sale as they are all dolled up on a plate and served after an elegant meal. Dress them up with a necklace of raspberries, or serve them no-frills, stacked one on top of the other for easy access. No matter how you present them, virtually everyone loves them…and for those few who don't, the recipes in this book should convince them of what they're missing!

Initially, I set out to develop over 50 brownie recipes, each one different and unique. I was determined not to get too weird either, because what's the point? How often are you going to bake Wasabi Brownies? Or Lemon Grass Brownies? Sure, as a once-in-a-while show-stopper you might, but I wanted recipes you would return to again and again—and more importantly, crave again and again.

It rapidly became difficult to create recipes that were distinctly different from one another and that fit into my original mandate: deep, dark and delicious. Over the years, in and out of my restaurants, I have perfected a few brownie recipes that I adore: they are easy and fudgy, and also versatile, meaning I don't have to turn the batter into brownies every time.

Eventually, from using these wonderful batters, I have developed ways to recreate the richness of brownies in recipes as disparate as Brownie Curd and Brownie Blob Cookies. So now you'll find, in addition to many true brownie variations, recipes that aren't technically brownies per se but which will, nonetheless, deliver the intense chocolate flavor imparted by their muse, the Classic Brownie (page 42). Brownie Heaven, it turns out, can be found equally in a Peanut Butter Caramel Tart (page 150) or a Kaffir Lime and Ginger Pot de Crème (page 134).

All of the recipes are simple, but some have detailed instructions. If you're making something for the first time, it's helpful to have more rather than less detail. Some of the recipes consist of several individual components that need to be made either ahead of time or one right after the other. None demand a huge amount of prior baking experience. But please, read the recipes all the way through to the end before you start! I can't tell you how many times I've started a recipe only to find I lacked an ingredient, or the time, to finish it properly. Or worst of all, there are times I've realized to my horror that I've already added an ingredient without proper whipping, melting, halving, etc.!

Chapter One provides recipes for components that make dessert assembly quick and easy. With these recipes on hand in the fridge or freezer, you'll be able to assemble desserts in minutes.

Chapter Two has the fudgiest, richest brownie recipes on the planet. These aren't your normal brownies. Virtually all of them have firm but melting edges and interiors that verge on the molten when warm. The Fudge Factor (page 40) is a 1–4 scale indicating just how fudgy each brownie recipe is. Once at room temperature or chilled, the brownies firm up to an amazing, chewy, not overly sweet, fudgy consistency. Served with a dollop of vanilla ice cream, they're the best dessert there is. Period.

The last few chapters of the book use chocolate to create the soul-satisfying quality of brownies in puddings, cookies, pancakes, tarts and other recipes.

So what are you waiting for? Turn the page and get going! Don't forget to have fun and share the results with your friends, who will think you are a baking genius. But most of all, enjoy!

Brownie (and Other Baking) Basics

WHAT'S GOOD FOR THE GOOSE IS GOOD FOR THE GANDER, as the familiar saying goes. In this case, you could say what's good for brownies is good for baking in general. Basic brownies are just the first stepping stone to more complex recipes. Master these techniques and approaches to ingredients and you're on your way to being a competent and calm home baker.

INGREDIENTS

These days, cookbooks go into great detail about required ingredients. The beauty of brownies, and the recipes inspired by them, is that they don't ask for much: fresh unsalted butter, eggs and good-quality chocolate. I use unbleached flour (or, for pâte sucrée, regular pastry flour) as well as instant blend flour, the latter because it blends without lumps in a sticky batter, and the former simply because I prefer it. (Instant blend flour is available in your grocery's baking section as "Wondra.") Granulated white and light or dark brown sugar. Pure vanilla, no artificial flavors. Large fresh or organic eggs. Fresh nuts, mostly lightly toasted and cooled before chopping. Whipping cream that is not ultra-pasteurized, because that really changes the flavor and slows the whipping. Seasonal fruit because it tastes better and is cheaper. Kosher salt because it brings out the flavor of chocolate like nothing else. (There are times when I sprinkle salt on top of my brownies for the most intense chocolate experience ever. Go ahead, try it! You'll be amazed at the difference in taste.)

CHOCOLATE

There's so much great-quality chocolate on the market that I won't recommend one over another, except to say that Scharffen Berger 99% unsweetened chocolate is the best in its class, and is all I use, because of its superior flavor. Still, you can use any supermarket, unsweetened chocolate as a replacement, but check the label before you buy your chocolate and don't buy anything that has sugar as the first ingredient, or that includes the artificial vanilla flavor, vanillin (not only because it doesn't taste good but because no one knows how to pronounce it properly). Scharffen Berger, Ghirardelli, Callebaut, Schokinag, Lindt, Valrhona—these are all chocolates that work well in my recipes as long as you use unsweetened, bittersweet or milk chocolate, as specified.

Most of the time, I use bittersweet chocolate with a 64% cocoa content, but you can use up to 70%. The higher the cocoa percentage and the cocoa butter content, the richer the taste, but you'll have to make some recipe adjustments. Should you find yourself with only a 70% chocolate and in desperate need of making one of the recipes, adjust your sugar upwards a bit and your butter down, to take into account the higher cocoa butter content in some of these intense chocolates. Brownies are incredibly sturdy and won't wilt with recipe tinkering, although they may ooze some butter while baking, or never completely firm up until refrigerated, so that you may not get what you expected. But 99% of the time, you get something delectable, even if it wasn't exactly what you anticipated. (For the best discussion yet on the characteristics and performance of various kinds of chocolate, read Alice Medrich's book, *Bittersweet*.)

As a hasty baker, I'm always looking for shortcuts. Melting chocolate, however, isn't one of the places where one should try to speed things up. Chocolate burns easily if set directly over heat, so my preferred methods are as follows.

MICROWAVE: Place chopped chocolate (yes, a pain, but in the end worth it in the reduction of melting time) in a glass bowl about 50% bigger than the amount of chocolate. Place in the microwave and melt on 50% power. The amount of time will depend upon the amount of chocolate you're melting. Set the time for a minute and check to see how much has melted. If most has melted, I generally let the residual heat melt the rest by giving it a stir. Otherwise, it goes back into the microwave for about 30 seconds. If I'm in a real hurry, I might microwave on 100% power but for no longer than 30-second increments, stirring after each.

STOVETOP: Heat a pot of simmering, not boiling, water. You'll need a bowl that fits snugly into the top of the pot and doesn't touch the water. Stainless steel works the fastest. Place the chocolate in the bowl and watch carefully. When most of the chocolate is melted, remove the bowl and stir, allowing the residual heat to do the rest of the work.

Under no circumstances should you allow any water or steam to come into contact with melted chocolate. It will "seize," which means it will clump up and become totally unusable. Don't even think about using it again. Throw it out and start over.

equipment

Brownies are wonderfully versatile from the standpoint of equipment: round, square and rectangular pans all work. In these recipes, you can use an 8-inch square (20-cm), a 9-inch square (23-cm), a 9- x 13-inch (23- x 33-cm) or a 10-inch (25-cm) round pan.

For the most part, I've chosen three pan sizes for my brownies. This doesn't mean that you can't make them in a round pan or even a smaller or larger pan, it just means that you'll have to adjust baking times because you'll either get a thicker or thinner brownie. My recipes for brownies tend to be large, and while you may certainly bake them off all at once, you don't have to do so, since the batter refrigerates and freezes wonderfully for months! As for the number of brownies in each recipe, that depends: brownies like these are very rich; therefore, a little goes a long way. In the recommended 9- x 9-inch (23-cm) pan, you could get as few as 9 or as many as 25! It all depends upon what you want to use them for, the main attraction or one of several.

Always line your pans with enough parchment paper to overhang the short sides of the pan and leave you with enough to grip. Let the brownies cool completely before lifting them out of the pan. Run a knife around the edges and they should come up easily. If chilled, the brownies may stick to the pan. In this case, set the pan over low heat on your stove, moving it from side to side for about 20 seconds, and the brownie slab will lift right out. Remember, too, to grease the sides with vegetable spray.

Many non-stick cookie sheets are just that, and won't need either paper liner or spray, but if you don't have non-stick sheets, I urge you to get yourself a roll of parchment paper. Don't throw it away after every use.

Just wipe it clean, let it dry, and set it flat in a drawer until you bake again. Silpat or other pan liners are also good, especially for Tuile Cookies (page 112). Although expensive, the liners last virtually forever and are well worth the investment.

BAKING

Since many of these recipes may make more brownie batter than you need, fill your pans three quarters of the way to the top, storing what is left over in the fridge or the freezer. Brownie batter is almost indestructible and has a long shelf life, thanks to the high proportion of sugar and fat, both preservatives. I have never had brownie batter go moldy.

There's no need to adjust your baking times or temperatures unless you've poured the batter far deeper than usual. In that case, simply add time in the form of 5-minute increments until you see the tell-tale signs of brownie perfection: risen sides, barely firm but not liquid center. It's always better to err on the side of underbaking brownies rather than overbaking them. If the times don't work for you as directed in the recipes, make sure your oven is working at the designated temperature by using an oven thermometer, or adjust the times to reflect whether your oven is too hot (reduce the heat and lower the rack) or too cold (increase the heat, raise the rack). No matter what, don't leave your baking, at least the first time you make a recipe, to chance. Keep an eye on it by looking at it through the oven window, and once in a while, open the door and jiggle the pan to see how it's coming along. It's not a cake or a soufflé where sudden moves may wreck the whopping 10 minutes it took you to put it together!

Baking is an exact art when it comes to the chemistry of ingredients but it can be inexact in the timing of the actual baking. Fluctuating humidity can affect baking times, as can the color of your pans and your oven temperature. What's more, your expectation of the recipe outcome may not be what the author intended.

What is commonly thought of as a brownie is definitely not what I intend in my recipes. My brownies are intended to be fudgy rather than cakey. However, the beauty of my recipes is that they're flexible. If you prefer them less fudgy, just bake them a few more minutes. At the same time, you have to exercise some judgment when you make any recipe for the first time: is the outcome to my liking and, if not, what can I do to get it where I want it? With some recipes, it's simply not possible, but happily, in most of these brownie recipes (not so much for other recipes), you can adjust baking times to affect outcome. Just be aware that the more you heat chocolate, the more chocolate flavor you lose because the compounds that create chocolate's flavor are highly volatile when heated.

Brownies are ready, according to my taste, when the edges are firm and the center is slightly puffed but jiggly without being liquid underneath the surface.

As they cool, the brownies continue to bake and the center firms up. If you slice them a half hour out of the oven, most of the fudgier brownies (see Fudge Factor on page 40) will have a range of brownie textures within the pan: the edges will slice well and hold their shape while the center pieces may actually ooze a little bit. If this is too gooey for you, just increase the baking time by 5-minute increments until you reach the texture you prefer, being aware that for the center to be firm, the edges will be firmer still. Or, follow my instructions and let the brownies cool completely to room temperature and/or refrigerate them, at which point the center will no longer be oozy, but it will certainly be fudgy. With my recipes, you won't get cakey brownies no matter how long you bake them! There are recipes for chocolate cakes with a deep brownie taste that you can bake into squares, but these are not, to my mind, true brownies.

And finally, use all your senses to determine doneness: if your kitchen has an intoxicating smell of chocolate, you know the brownies should be ready soon; if a toothpick put into the center comes out covered with batter, you know it has a way to go, but if it comes out with a few crumbs on it, then it's all but ready. Watch the stages of baking as they occur: the top gets shiny, then begins to look puffy and matte with the feel of liquid batter underneath when you tap it, while halfway through baking, the edges will be firm, the center will start to rise and even crack a little, but underneath will be jelly-like. When you remove the brownies from the oven, the center will fall, creating the luscious denseness these brownies are famous for.

In the end, these recipes are for you and what you like so don't be afraid to experiment. There's really not much you can do to ruin most of them unless you burn them— in which case, I'd say you've probably overbaked them!

fudge factor

To convey the difference between my brownies and more traditional ones, I've created a Fudge Factor scale of 1–4 (see page 40). The ratings next to each recipe tell you how comparitively moist and fudgy each brownie will be. The Classic Brownie and Bar None stand as paragons of brownie fudginess. All else is rated against them. At room temperature, edges will be slightly crisp but towards the center of the slab, the brownie will be increasingly soft to the touch, verging on molten. Chilled, the center will firm up and be dense with chocolate without the overwhelming sweetness of fudge. At no time will these brownies be cakey or have much of a crumb. They're stubbornly rich and decadent and proud of it

storage

Among the many attributes that make brownies wonderful, ease and length of storage are foremost.

Virtually all the recipes in this book have longer storage potential than regular baked goods. In general, consume recipes with fruit the same day they're made. Those without fruit can frequently be refrigerated and frozen with little, if any, loss in quality. Just make sure you wrap everything first in plastic and then in foil. Put soft and sticky items, like cheesecake brownies, on a cardboard base and then wrap them. Don't forget to identify and date them since your freezer will quickly fill up with foil packages of various shapes and sizes; you think you'll remember what's in them but a week later, they will all look alarmingly the same. Having a well-stocked freezer is, however, a sign that you're on your way to being a great pastry chef, with fully prepared and partially completed items ready to finish at a moment's notice.

Keeping brownies in the fridge intensifies their fudge-like qualities. However, cold masks their deep, rich flavor, so serving them slightly warm might sacrifice texture but definitely enhances flavor. Fifteen to 20 seconds in the microwave is enough to warm up a brownie perfectly.

weights and measures

When I was a kid, there was this puzzle: Which weighs more, a pound of feathers or a pound of lead? Most of us would choose lead until we realized that a pound is a pound whether it's made of feathers, lead or chocolate. How much space (volume) one pound of lead would take up, compared to a pound of feathers, is another story. And would that pound of feathers always take up the same amount of room or slightly more or less depending upon how fluffy it was?

All this is to explain why professional cooks use weight as the preferred method of portioning their ingredients. Time after time, 180 g or 10 oz. (by weight) of cocoa is the same whether it's packed, tamped, sifted or scooped, whereas a cup (by volume) of cocoa is a good 10 g or almost ½ oz., less if it's sifted versus scooped. The same goes for flour, a critical ingredient in most of these recipes. Variations in flour weight can affect the outcome so the result is never the same—sometimes too dense, other times not dense enough. The key is to have a delicious recipe, time after time, and weighing ingredients rather than measuring helps to achieve this.

This is also why recipes differentiate between such things as "1 cup nuts, chopped" and "1 cup chopped nuts." The first asks you to measure your nuts then chop them. The second, to chop some nuts and then measure. Chopped nuts take up less room than nut pieces so you can get a lot more into a cup. Therefore, 1 cup chopped nuts will weigh differently than the same *volume* of whole nuts.

When you make a recipe a second time, it will be difficult (but not impossible) to duplicate exactly what you did the first time unless you weigh ingredients. Despite this, most cookbooks call for volumetric measures, such as cups or milliliters. This works fine, most of the time, but if you want consistency, invest in a small kitchen scale (digital if possible) and you'll never look back. You'll soon become acquainted with the conversion of volume measures to their weight equivalents. Furthermore, you'll be surprised at how inaccurate measuring cups and spoons can be. I have different styles of measuring cups and spoons and each one holds a different amount of sugar, so it's no wonder my baking results varied until I converted to weighing ingredients. Keep in mind, though, that it's difficult to weigh small amounts, which is why anything from about 2 Tbsp (30 mL) and under is given by volume in my recipes.

"The metric system." Say these words to most Americans and they cringe. As someone who grew up with ounces and pounds, and who came to Canada just as the metric system was mandated into law, I can tell you it's so much easier to use than the Imperial system. Based on 1000 g to a kilo, which is equivalent to 1 litre of water or 1000 mL, everything else just falls into place. Think of a pound of butter as slightly less (454 g) than half a kilo; think of the 5 cups of sugar (200 g each) that makes a kilo and you'll be able to determine whether that 5-pound (2.25-kg) bag of sugar holds enough for you to make two batches of brownies. Flour is a bit trickier: some pastry chefs use 140 g as their 1-cup equivalent, while I use 130 g. This doesn't matter too much if you adhere to the recipe as shown, but if you decide to expand the recipe by multiplying it tenfold, then that minor 10 g difference can be the difference between the recipe being faithful to the original or becoming something different and not altogether that pleasing. This is another reason to use weight as your preferred portioning method. When you decide that you need four times the recipe, you'll guarantee with 4 x 100 g that each time you'll get 400 g, not 379 g or 412 g.

For those who are still not convinced that metric (and weight) is a superior system, here's a conversion chart for some of the main ingredients in this book.

INGREDIENT	MEASURE	GRAMS	OUNCES
Granulated sugar	1 cup (250 mL)	200	7
Brown sugar	1 cup (250 mL)	220	8
Icing sugar	1 cup (250 mL)	120	4
All-purpose flour	1 cup (250 mL)	130	4½
Whole wheat flour	1 cup (250 mL)	130	4½
Chocolate, chip-sized pieces	1 cup (250 mL)	175	16
Raisins	1 cup (250 mL)	120	4
Butter	1 cup (250 mL)	227	8
Peanut butter	1 cup (250 mL)	227	8
Whole nuts (average)	1 cup (250 mL)	120	4¼
Eggs, large	1 each	50	1¾

PERFECT BARS EVERY TIME: SLICE YOUR BROWNIES LIKE A PRO

Have you ever wondered how bakery brownies are so perfectly cut? I did too until I worked in a bakery. There are two ways to do it.

The old-fashioned way is to measure very carefully with a ruler. First, we trimmed the edges, saving them for either rum balls or afternoon snacks. Then we scored the brownie slab at even intervals both vertically and horizontally. We dipped a BIG, sharp chef's knife in hot water and wiped it dry, then made a single slice from one end of the knife to the other. Because the brownie slab was bigger than the knife, it took a few slices. And because the brownie was sticky, after each slice we dipped the knife into hot water and wiped it again before the next slice. This would keep the edge of the brownies, especially iced ones, perfectly vertical and sharp.

One day, we got a nifty gadget that looked like an expanding child safety gate with wheels on the ends. We could expand or contract it to create the intervals we wanted, vertically and horizontally, and roll the wheels, which would score the brownies evenly. This saved an incredible amount of time and produced perfect brownies every time. Alas, these cutters are expensive for the home baker, so I suggest using the old-fashioned ruler and chef knife method. (However, if this accordion cutter intrigues you, it can be found at professional baking and restaurant supply stores.)

To slice professional-looking bars, invert the baked, chilled brownie slab onto a metal cooling rack. Place both rack and slab on a cookie sheet lined with parchment paper. Pour warm glaze (not hot—if it's too hot it will run off the sides and be absorbed by the brownie, which you don't want) over the center of the brownie slab until you have a pool that runs the width of the slab. Use an offset spatula to gently nudge or push the glaze down to, and over, the ends. You're not frosting the brownie slab but glazing it, so a gentle touch will keep the glaze shiny and smooth. If there's not enough glaze to make it to the ends, simply pour some more over the top. If you feel daring and the rack isn't too big, pick up both rack and brownie slab and tip it in the direction that you want the glaze to flow. Don't worry about all the glaze you're using. It will fall onto the parchment paper where you can scoop it up easily when it's cooled, strain it and place in a plastic container for future use. This isn't a time to skimp. Beautiful glazing requires lots of glaze to do the job. Place in the fridge to chill thoroughly, about 2 hours.

Run a sharp chef's knife under hot water to heat it, then dry thoroughly. Remove the rough edges and measure the slab, scoring it at even intervals. Place the tip of the knife at one end and firmly cut down into the brownie. Draw the knife through the bar without bringing it up through the glaze. This will guarantee a straight edge. Remove the knife, run it under hot water and wipe it dry. Repeat with each cut.

BROWNIE offspring

A recent conversation with one of my editors, Alison, reminded me that most people, when they have a baking failure, simply discard the mess and start over or vow never to make that recipe again.

Alison was bemoaning the fact that a brownie recipe from a prominent chef's book didn't turn out and she had poured $15 worth of fancy chocolate into it. The problem was overcooked edges and a gooey center. "What did you do with it?" I asked. "I threw it out," she replied. I was aghast. There's so much you can do with brownie batter that you should never throw it out unless you have burned it. (For that, there really is no cure.)

So, Alison, these tricks of the trade are for you. Professional chefs rarely throw anything out. Here are a few things to do with stale, overcooked or underdone brownies, brownies you thought were so-so but not up to snuff—or just too damn many of them!

MUSHY/GREASY BROWNIES

This is often the result of too little baking time, too much sugar or butter or substitution of a higher percentage chocolate, or omission of a key ingredient, like eggs (it happens).

Return the pan to the oven and bake another 5–10 minutes at 300ºF (150ºC). The edges might overcook but these can easily be trimmed. If this doesn't fix the problem, proceed to the next step.

Place the brownies in the fridge to see if they'll firm up. If so, eat them!

If refrigeration doesn't do the trick, and your brownies are still liquidy, place the whole mess in the mixing bowl of an electric mixer fitted with the paddle attachment.

Beat the hell out of them, until you have a fairly smooth mixture. It won't be like new but it will have character! Add 1–2 eggs, and beat until smooth. Pour into a parchment-lined brownie pan and bake at 300ºF (150ºC) for 30–40 minutes. Or, pour into a cake pan, cover with foil, and place in a hot water bath and bake until firm, about an hour. You'll now have Brownie Pudding.

If you don't want to rebake, soften a quart of ice cream and fold the brownie mixture into it. Voila! You have created Brownie Ripple Ice Cream.

OVERBAKED BROWNIES

These tend to be dry, not the texture you were after. Often there's a 1-inch (2.5-cm) perimeter of tough, crisp crust, while the center of the brownie is great. Simply trim the edges and save them.

Use the trimmed edges or the whole mess of overbaked brownies to make Brownie Crumble Topping. Rub the brownies between your hands over a bowl to create rough, large crumbs. Place them on a cookie sheet and dry out in a 250ºF (120ºC) oven for about 20 minutes, tossing from time to time. When you're ready to use them as topping, they can either go on as is, or, for a fruit crumble, moisten them with some melted butter and plop them on top of your fruit; or use them to make triscotti (page 104).

Brownie crumble makes a great snack for kids; just serve it as is, or mix it in with some nuts and raisins.

Fold the crumble into chocolate ice cream with some bananas and nuts for your own version of Chunky Monkey!

BROWNIE POINT: *mise en place*

You'll find Brownie Points throughout the book. These are helpful hints for working with brownies or adapting a particular recipe for a variety of uses.

The single most useful brownie point is *mise en place.*

Mise en place is French for "to put in place," or Get Organized! It is a practice used by all professional cooks. In fact, if you watch chefs on television, all those little dishes are nothing more than a *mise en place*. Without it, you (like the TV chefs) risk forgetting an ingredient, and/or making assembly more complicated and time-consuming than necessary. It's a way of organizing yourself so that baking (and cooking) can become a series of simple steps, accomplished by taking your prepared ingredients and putting them together as detailed in the recipe. It also assures consistency of results, time after time.

Here's how you set up your *mise en place*.

- Read the recipe from start to finish.

- Measure or weigh out all your ingredients and place them in bowls on your work surface so you can be sure you haven't forgotten anything.

- Process the ingredients as required: bring your eggs to room temperature, zest your lemons, toast your nuts, melt your butter, etc., so you aren't scrambling at the last minute to get that lemon zested while your batter sits, deflating.

Once you become accustomed to using this technique, you'll find that every recipe becomes much faster to produce.

An aspect of *mise en place* that every pastry chef uses is having a larder stocked with component parts which, when assembled, make knockout desserts in a matter of minutes. This means that you may have to take an hour or two one rainy day to make some basic recipes, but in sacrificing this initial time, you'll have saved yourself endless future hours of assembling a cookie dough or waiting for ganache to cool or pastry to chill.

You're now ready to go. Chapter One provides you with some great recipes to fill your larder so you can quickly assemble the recipes in the later chapters. Not one of these recipes takes more than 15 minutes to make. With all or some of these items available, you'll be able to assemble desserts at a moment's notice that will leave your family and friends not only begging for more but wondering how you were able to do it without breaking out into hives of anxiety!

Or, if you prefer, just jump in and go straight to Chapter Two where the brownies are. Don't forget to lick the bowl and have fun!

THE CLASSIC BROWNIE p. 42   WITH GANACHE p. 28

left: peanut butter caramel tart   p. 150
this page: the classic brownie p. 42

clockwise, from left: BROWNIE BLOBS p. 117, ULTIMATE, ULTIMATE CHOCOLATE CHUNK COOKIES p. 103, CHOCOLATE RUGELAH p. 118, HALVAH BROWNIE COOKIES p. 110

Brownie Building Blocks

1

shiny chocolate glaze

YIELD: SCANT 2 CUPS (500 mL)

This is a sensational chocolate glaze that stays shiny whether refrigerated or not. Freeze it but don't refrigerate it for longer than a few weeks or it may grow green furry things that are only suitable for your kid's science project.

½ cup	125 mL	coffee or water
⅓ cup	65 g	sugar
6 oz	160 g	bittersweet chocolate, chopped
2 Tbsp	30 mL	corn syrup
2 Tbsp	30 mL	butter
2 tsp	10 mL	coffee or vanilla extract

1. Over medium heat, warm the coffee or water, sugar and chocolate in a medium saucepan.

2. Add the corn syrup and bring to a boil. Boil for 5 minutes, stirring once or twice.

3. Remove from the heat. Add the butter and coffee or vanilla extract.

4. Pour into a bowl. Let cool to room temperature, at which point it will thicken. If you pour it over a cake before it has cooled, it will slide off! If it thickens too much, place over hot water to warm gently.

BROWNIE POINT

This makes a great base for a quick and easy hot chocolate. Heat milk and stir in 2 heaping tablespoonfuls of glaze. Top with marshmallows!

pâte sucrée

YIELD: MAKES 4 9-INCH (23-CM) FLAN SHELLS

This is the recipe that M. Seurre gave me when I left my "stage" apprenticeship in Paris. Every day I would arrive, eager as ever, with my little notebook and turquoise pen, ready to copy down as many recipes as I could during our "pause café" of instant coffee, because the rest of the time they worked me tirelessly and I was happy to oblige. On my last day, the crew presented me with a wonderful book with all their recipes neatly typed but, as is typical of professionals, with no instructions. I always have a disc of both this dough and its chocolate version in my freezer, ready to defrost at a moment's notice when I see wonderful fruit in the store. This is a large quantity; if you want a smaller amount, divide the recipe by 4 and use a single egg.

1 lb + 4 Tbsp	500 g	butter, cold
2 cups	240 g	icing sugar
3		eggs
7 ¾ cups	1 kg	pastry flour
1 tsp	5 mL	baking powder
		pinch kosher salt

1. Cut the butter into 32 pieces and place in the bowl of an electric mixer fitted with the paddle attachment.

2. Add the icing sugar and toss to coat the butter.

3. On low speed, mix the butter and the sugar together until blended. Scrape the bottom of the bowl.

4. Add the eggs one at a time, on low speed, scraping the bowl often.

5. Add the remaining dry ingredients and mix until the dough just comes together. It may be a bit sticky.

6. Turn the dough out onto a lightly floured surface and gently knead it for about 30 seconds.

7. Divide it into four pieces, press into flat discs and wrap individually in plastic. Refrigerate until firm before rolling.

8. If freezing, wrap in foil. If you have extra flan pans, line the bottom and sides with rolled dough, wrap the pan first in plastic and then foil and freeze. When ready to use, defrost in the fridge and bake as directed in your recipe.

9. Remove the dough from the fridge about 15 minutes before you want to roll it. When you are ready to roll out the disc, lightly flour your work surface. If you need the dough in a hurry, take the cold disc and gently pound it from side to side with a rolling pin. This will soften it enough to roll.

10. Roll the dough to slightly larger than the diameter of the pan plus two times the height. For a 9- x 4-inch (23- x 10-cm) rectangular pan, for example, roll it to about 11 x 6 inches (28 x 15 cm). For a 9-inch (23-cm) round pan, roll it into a circle of about 11 inches (28 cm) in diameter.

11. Fold the dough in half and lay it in the middle of the pan. Unfold and gently press the dough down the sides to meet the bottom at a right angle. If there are thin areas along the sides, fold or press any excess dough down into the sides to increase the thickness. If the sides are too thick, press the dough against the side of the pan to thin it. Use a paring knife set at an angle to trim the crust flush with the top of the pan.

13. Place in the fridge to chill completely, at least 30 minutes, before baking.

14. Depending upon your recipe, use as is or bake blind. To blind bake, preheat the oven to 350°F (180°C). Prick the bottom pastry all over with a fork, line the pastry with foil and fill with dried beans or other weights. Bake for about 10–15 minutes (or as detailed in the recipe) until lightly golden brown, if further baking is required after it is filled. Bake completely to a rich, golden brown if the shell is to be filled after baking.

15. Cool before filling.

BROWNIE POINTS

When rolling dough, use a large, flat metal spatula or removable bottom of a flan pan to loosen the dough from the work surface before turning the dough or sprinkling more flour beneath it. This way you won't tear the pastry when you move it.

The dough is easiest to work with when it's cool and almost leathery in feel. If it gets too warm and sticky, place the rolled portion on a cookie sheet and refrigerate until chilled enough to roll.

BROWNIE SANDWICH COOKIES

Roll one round of dough to ⅛-inch (2-mm) thickness. Use a cookie cutter with a 2-inch (5-cm) diameter to cut out rounds. Using the small end of a large, plain piping tube, cut out the middle of half the rounds (or omit this step altogether). Roll out the scraps from the middles for additional cookies. Place all the rounds on a parchment-lined baking pan and bake at 350°F (180°C) for about 10 minutes or until barely golden brown around the edges. Cool. Turn the circles without holes upside down. Pipe or spoon 1 tsp (5 mL) of Brownie Curd (page 24) into the middle of the rounds. Dust the tops with holes with a good coating of icing sugar. Place them on top of the Brownie Curd. Some of the filling will ooze into the hole, but that's how you want it!

pâte sucrée au chocolat

YIELD: MAKES 6 4-INCH (10-CM) TARTLETS OR 2 8-INCH (20-CM) FLANS.

This chocolate version isn't very sweet but provides a pleasant sharpness for the fillings suggested below. The dough gets sticky when it warms up. Roll it between 2 pieces of parchment paper (or Silpat liners) to make handling easier. If it gets too soft, just return the dough, between the pieces of paper, to the fridge. Let it firm up before rolling or cutting.

10 Tbsp	140 g	**butter**
¾ cup	90 g	**icing sugar**
1 Tbsp	10 g	**granulated sugar**
1		**egg yolk**
1 ¾ cups	210 g	**pastry flour**
½ cup	60 g	**cocoa**
		pinch kosher salt

1. Cut the butter into 10 pieces (if not already in tablespoons) and place in the bowl of an electric mixer fitted with the paddle attachment.

2. Add both sugars and toss to coat the butter.

3. On low speed, mix the butter and sugars together until blended. Scrape the bottom of the bowl.

4. Add the egg yolk on low speed, and scrape the bowl.

5. Whisk the flour, cocoa and salt together.

6. Add to the butter mixture and blend until the dough just comes together. It may be a bit sticky.

7. Press into a flat disc and wrap in plastic. Refrigerate for at least 30 minutes before using.

8. If freezing, wrap in plastic and then foil. Or line a flan pan with the rolled dough, wrap it in plastic and foil and freeze. It will be ready at a moment's notice when you need it.

9. When you are ready to roll out the disc, lightly flour your work surface. Remove the dough from the fridge about 15 minutes before you want to roll it.

10. Roll the dough to about 2 inches (5 cm) larger than the diameter of your tart pan.

11. Fold the dough in half and lay it in the middle of the pan. Unfold and gently press the dough down the sides to meet the bottom at a right angle. If there are thin areas along the sides, fold or press any excess dough down into the sides to increase the thickness. If the sides are too thick, press the dough against the side of the pan to thin it. Use a paring knife set at an angle to trim the dough flush with the top of the pan.

12. Place in the fridge to chill completely, at least 30 minutes, before baking.

13. Depending on your recipe, use as is or bake blind. To blind bake, preheat the oven to 350°F (180°C). Prick the bottom of the pastry all over with a fork, line the pastry with foil and fill with dried beans or other weights. Bake for about 10–15 minutes (or as detailed in the recipe) until it looks and feels firm. Chocolate pastry is notoriously difficult to gauge but it's always better to underbake than overbake.

14. Cool before filling.

CHOCOLATE SANDWICH COOKIES

Instead of patting the dough into a disc, roll it into a log 1 ½ inches (4 cm) in diameter. Wrap roll in plastic, then foil, label and freeze. When you need a quick cookie, slice into ⅛-inch (2-mm) rounds and bake at 325°F (160°C) for 8–10 minutes or until just crisp around the edges. Cool and pipe or spread Brownie Curd (page 24) on the bottom of one cookie. Top with a second cookie. Dust with icing sugar.

DÉLICE AU CHOCOLAT

Roll the dough to ⅛-inch (2-mm) thickness. Use a 3-inch (7.5-cm) scalloped cookie cutter to cut out 6 discs. Bake at 350°F (180°C) for 8–10 minutes. Cool. Pipe Brownie Curd (page 24), as is or lightened with some whipped cream, or whipped Ganache (page 28) into the center, leaving some room at the edges. Place fresh raspberries in a circle around the edges. Top with another cookie and press down slightly. Pipe a rosette of filling on top and press a fresh raspberry and mint leaf in at a rakish angle. Dust lightly with icing sugar.

KEY LIME CHOCOLATE TARTS

Roll out 6 4-inch (10-cm) tart shells, line with foil and weight with beans. Bake until ¾ done (about 10 minutes for small tarts; 12–15 minutes for larger tarts). While they're baking, whisk together 2 eggs, 1 egg yolk, ¾ cup + 2 Tbsp sugar (175 g), 3 Tbsp (45 mL) key lime juice, ½ tsp (2 mL) baking powder and ¼ tsp (1 mL) salt. Fill each tart shell almost to the brim. Bake in a 300°F (150°C) oven for about 20 minutes or until the filling is no longer liquid. Sprinkle the top with toasted coconut.

BROWNIE CURD

YIELD: SCANT 2 CUPS (500 mL)

There's lemon curd and lime curd, and there's vanilla custard and chocolate custard, but no one, to my knowledge, has ever created a brownie curd! Gorgeously dark and not too sweet, this is a wonderful spread on cinnamon toast, a filling for prebaked tart shells or Chocolate Brownie Cigars (page 111) or for making Brownie Tacos (page 112). Best of all, properly stored it has a long shelf life, so you can pull it out of the fridge and create something spontaneous with very little effort.

1 cup	250 mL	whipping cream
1		vanilla bean, sliced in half lengthwise
½ cup	60 g	cocoa
½ cup	100 g	sugar
3		egg yolks
1		whole egg
¼ tsp	1 mL	kosher salt
1 Tbsp	15 mL	butter
2 ½ oz	70 g	bittersweet chocolate, chopped

1. Place the cream and vanilla bean in a medium saucepan. Bring to a low simmer and turn off the heat. Let sit for 30 minutes.

2. Using the tip of a knife, scrape out the seeds from the bean into the cream. Remove the bean, rinse and place in your sugar jar to flavor your sugar.

3. Add the cocoa to the vanilla cream and whisk to blend.

4. Place the saucepan over medium heat and heat just until you see bubbles around the edges.

5. In another bowl, whisk together the sugar, egg yolks, egg and salt.

6. Gradually whisk the warm cream into the eggs and sugar (wrap a tea towel around the bottom of the bowl so the bowl doesn't move while you pour and whisk at the same time).

7. Place a sieve over the saucepan and pour the curd mixture back into the pan, discarding whatever is left in the sieve.

8. Return the pan to the heat and mix constantly with a wooden spoon. The mixture must not boil! Keep mixing until you feel and see the curd thickening. You will feel resistance to your stirring. From time to time, remove the pan from the heat and stir, keeping an eye on the mixture to make sure it's not boiling or burning on the bottom.

9. When the curd has thickened to the consistency of sour cream, remove from the heat and stir in the butter and chopped chocolate. Mix to blend thoroughly.

10. At this point, you may pour the curd directly into pre-baked tart shells (see Brownie Curd Raspberry Tarts) or place in a sealed container with a piece of plastic wrap set directly on the surface of the curd to keep it moist.

11. Store in the fridge for up to 3 weeks.

BROWNIE CURD RASPBERRY TARTS

Fill 6 4-inch (10-cm) baked Pâte Sucrée (page 20) or Pâte Sucrée au Chocolat tart shells (page 22) with warm Brownie Curd. Place fresh raspberries (about 1 pint) in concentric circles on top, starting from the outside edge and covering the entire surface. Dust lightly with icing sugar.

PEANUT BUTTER BROWNIE CURD SPREAD

Mix equal amounts of smooth peanut butter and Brownie Curd together. Make sure they are both at room temperature. Use as a filling for sandwich cookies (see Pâte Sucrée au Chocolat, page 22), or Rugelah (page 118).

BROWNIE CURD PRALINE SPREAD

Mix together equal amounts of praline paste (available from gourmet stores) and Brownie Curd. Use to fill cookies or tarts or fold it into whipped cream for a complex and utterly delicious mousse.

BROWNIE POINTS

Here are just a few suggestions for ways to use Brownie Curd.

Stir ¼ cup (60 mL) curd into a cup of hot milk (or better yet, hot cream!) for the best hot chocolate ever.

Mix ¼ cup (60 mL) curd with 3 Tbsp (45 mL) whipping cream to thin. Fold into 1 cup (250 mL) whipped cream for a quick mousse.

Mix ¾ cup (175 mL) curd with 2 Tbsp (30 mL) whipping cream. Pour into pre-baked tart shells and let set. Garnish with berries and/or crème fraîche.

Spread between layers of angel food cake.

Place curd in a small piping bag fitted with a #2 or #5 plain tip. Pipe into the hollow end of raspberries for an outrageously extravagant end to an elegant meal.

Mix with equal amounts of warmed raspberry jam for an extra-special breakfast spread.

mascarpone chocolate curd

YIELD: 4 ½ CUPS (1.125 L)

If you haven't already made the recipe for Brownie Curd (page 24), then shame on you! However, it's never too late. One of my testers said this recipe was so good that I should tell everyone to double it. So, go ahead, double it and give it away to your best friends or store it in the fridge where it will remain delicious for a long time, as long as you place plastic wrap flush with the top and seal it tightly in a container.

1 pound	450 g	bittersweet chocolate chips
2 cups	500 mL	mascarpone cheese or sour cream
5 Tbsp	70 g	butter
4		eggs, lightly beaten
		pinch kosher salt

1. Place the chocolate, mascarpone or sour cream and butter in a medium saucepan over low heat. Stir gently until it is all melted.

2. Remove the pan from the heat and quickly whisk in the eggs, being sure that you whisk briskly to incorporate them before they have a chance to cook and curdle.

3. Return the pan to low heat and stir until the mixture thickens, again being careful not to cook to the boiling point.

4. Pour the curd through a fine sieve into a bowl, using a rubber spatula to press it through.

5. Stir in the salt.

6. Store in a sealed container with a piece of plastic wrap flush with the surface of the curd to keep it moist. Refrigerate.

7. Reheat by placing it in a bowl over gently simmering water until it liquefies.

BROWNIE POINTS

Use as an ultra-rich pudding, all on its own.

Pour into espresso cups and chill or serve warm, topped with a swirl of sweetened whipped cream.

Spread between cake layers or cookies.

Fill meringue cups and surround with berries.

Make peanut butter and mascarpone curd french toast: mix equal amounts of brownie curd and peanut butter; sandwich between two pieces of egg bread; dip in beaten egg and fry until golden in lots of butter. Serve with fresh raspberries or a raspberry purée.

Any way you serve it, it is wonderful.

crème anglaise

YIELD: SCANT 3 CUPS (750 mL)

This is another recipe M. Seurre and his team gave me when I completed my apprenticeship at Patisserie Seurre. He was so generous with all his recipes that I feel it a duty to pass them on for others to enjoy. Use this as a sauce or garnish for everything from brownies to cakes to tarts and berries.

2 cups	500 mL	milk
1		vanilla bean, split lengthwise
4		egg yolks
⅔ cup	130 g	sugar

1. In a medium saucepan on medium heat, bring the milk and vanilla bean to just under a boil. You will see little bubbles around the edges. Steam will begin to rise from the surface.

2. Meanwhile, whisk together the egg yolks and sugar.

3. Pour ¼ of the hot milk into the egg yolk/sugar mixture, whisking rapidly so the eggs don't cook, but are heated through.

4. Pour the egg/milk mixture into the saucepan with the remaining milk and whisk to blend.

5. Return the pot to low heat and stir constantly with a wooden spoon until it begins to thicken. Do not let it boil or the eggs will cook and the mixture will curdle.

6. The cream is ready when you can run your finger across the back of the spoon and the cream remains in place on either side of the track.

7. Strain the cream into a clean bowl. Remove the vanilla bean. Use the tip of a knife to scrape all the seeds into the crème anglaise. (Rinse the vanilla bean and put it into your sugar bin for vanilla-infused sugar.)

8. Cover with plastic wrap pressed onto the surface of the crème to keep it moist. Seal tightly. Chill if not using immediately.

BROWNIE POINT

For flavored Crème Anglaise, omit the vanilla and replace with a tablespoonful of your favorite liqueur.

ganache

YIELD: 4 CUPS (1 L)

Ganache is French for a combination of cream and chocolate. It's one of the simplest things to make and one of the most versatile. It's also the filling and glaze for truffles. Make sure that you use cream as fresh as you can get it, preferably organic, and the best chocolate you can afford. Don't be afraid to experiment by infusing the hot cream with flavors like vanilla bean, grated ginger or cinnamon. Heat the cream, add the flavoring and let sit for an hour or so, then strain. You'll have to reheat the cream before completing the ganache. My ganache varies depending upon whether or not I want it thinner (add more cream or reduce the chocolate) or shiny (add some corn syrup), but it always starts with equal amounts of chocolate and cream by weight. I portion out the recipe into 4 containers, label and freeze them so I always have some glaze, or chocolate "sauce," available to jazz up a dessert.

2 cups	500 mL	**heavy cream**
1 pound	454 g	**bittersweet chocolate, chopped**

1. Heat the cream to just below a boil, when bubbles appear around the edges of the saucepan.

2. Pour it over the chopped chocolate and let sit for 5 minutes.

3. Gently whisk until smooth. Try not to create air bubbles.

4. To use as a glaze, cool (or reheat) to between 80° and 85°F (27–30°C).

BROWNIE POINTS

Ganache is incredibly versatile. To use it as mousse, make recipe omitting corn syrup and coffee. Place in the fridge until cold but not solid and beat with the whisk attachment of an electric mixer until light and fluffy. Don't overmix or it will become grainy. You want it smooth. Use as you would a mousse: as a cake filling, as a base for a parfait, as a filling between cookies.

For truffle filling, use a 2:1 ratio of chocolate to cream and add ¼ of the weight of the chocolate in butter. Pour into a parchment-lined jelly roll pan and refrigerate until completely firm. Using a teaspoon or a scoop, form into balls and place on another parchment-lined sheet. Refrigerate until firm. Roll quickly into balls and return to the fridge. Roll in cocoa, chopped nuts or icing sugar or dip into melted but cooled chocolate.

To use as chocolate sauce, reheat gently in a hot water bath. Flavor with liqueur and serve over ice cream and brownies to make a Brownie Sundae.

For glaze, let your brownies (or cake) cool in the pan, then chill completely. Pour the ganache on top and tilt the pan so the ganache covers the top completely and evenly. Let cool. Dip a tea towel in hot water and squeeze it dry. Wrap it around the edges of the pan. When the ganache starts melting around the edges, lift out the brownie slab or open the springform surrounding the cake. You will have clean edges. Slice with a hot knife wiped clean after every cut.

For a professional gloss and expert finishing touch, drizzle ganache over cookies, cakes, and pies (such as pecan).

Put warm ganache into a squeeze bottle and make wonderful designs by spreading Crème Anglaise (page 27) on serving plate and drizzling concentric ganache circles over top. Use a toothpick or knife tip to "pull" the chocolate from the center towards the edges of the plate at 1-inch (3-cm) intervals. Place your dessert in the center of this "web."

Vary the flavors of your ganache by reducing the cream by a tablespoon or two and substituting liqueurs such as Grand Marnier (orange), Kahlua (coffee), or even straight whisky or rum. Don't be afraid to experiment!

Infuse your cream first with exotic spice blends: simmer the cream with 1 Tbsp (15 mL) chai tea spices or 2 cinnamon sticks or 2 tsp (10 mL) Earl Grey tea and let sit for about 15 minutes. Return to just below the boil and strain over the chocolate. Whisk until smooth.

crème d'amande

This classic French filling is a recipe you'll use again and again, and not just with brownies. It can be doubled or tripled and frozen for up to a year. This makes a large quantity but you can easily halve it.

½ pound	227 g	butter, at room temperature
½ pound	227 g	sugar
½ pound	227 g	ground almonds
3		eggs at room temperature, lightly beaten
1 tsp	5 mL	almond extract

1. Place the butter in the bowl of an electric mixer fitted with the paddle attachment. Beat until softened, about 3 minutes.

2. With the machine on low speed add the sugar. Increase the speed to medium and beat until light and fluffy, about 4 minutes. Scrape down the sides and bottom as required.

3. Add the ground almonds and beat just until incorporated.

4. With the machine on low speed, add the eggs in a slow but steady stream. Scrape the sides and bottom of the bowl.

5. Add the almond extract. Increase the speed to medium and beat until light and fluffy.

6. Use immediately, or store in a covered container in the freezer.

chocolate frangipane fresh berry tart

Line a 7.5-inch (19-cm) tart pan with Pâte Sucrée au Chocolat (page 22). (You will need about ½ the recipe.) Prick with a fork. Line with foil and weight with beans or weights to keep the pastry from shrinking. Bake at 350°F (180°C) for 12 minutes. Remove the foil and weights. Spread ¾ cup (175 mL) of the crème filling to ¼ inch (5 mm) below the top. Press ½ pint fresh raspberries into the crème. Return to the oven and bake until the filling is slightly puffed and set, about 20–25 minutes. Cool. Warm ½ cup (125 mL) Ganache (page 28). Pour over the top of the cooled tart and tip and turn the tart gently so the chocolate covers the entire surface. Serve as is or generously cover the surface either neatly or randomly with fresh raspberries. Dust with icing sugar and serve.

hazelnut cherry chocolate tart

Make the crème, substituting toasted, peeled hazelnuts for the almonds. Line a 7.5-inch (19-cm) tart pan with Pâte Sucrée (page 20). Prick with a fork. Line with foil and beans or weights to keep the pastry from shrinking. Bake at 350°F (180°C) for 12 minutes. Remove the foil and weights. Spread ¾ cup (175 mL) of the crème filling to ¼ inch (5 mm) below the top. Dot the filling with fresh, pitted sour cherries. Sprinkle with cinnamon sugar and return to the oven until the crème is barely firm and slightly golden brown, about 20–25 minutes. Drizzle the top with Ganache (page 28) and let it set. Dust with icing sugar.

brownies à la crème

Swirl ½ cup (125 mL) of the crème into your favorite brownie recipe. Top with ½ cup (60 g) almonds, sliced and tossed gently in a lightly beaten egg white and a tablespoon (15 mL) of granulated sugar. Bake at 300°F (150°C) for approximately 30-40 minutes or until it's slightly puffed in the center and the top is golden with shiny almonds. Voila! A dense, moist center with a crispy, crackly topping.

caramel butterscotch sauce

YIELD: SCANT 2 CUPS (500 mL)

When I was a kid, I could never decide which sauce was better, a gooey caramel, with its rich buttery undertones, or hot fudge, so I usually had both. This and the Chocolate Fudge Sauce (page 34) are among my favorite recipes because they can be used over ice cream, in brownies or drizzled on a plate to dazzle your friends and wow your family. You can personalize this recipe by deciding to what degree you like your sugar caramelized: really dark, it gets a bitter edge that some people crave; golden, and the flavor is less pronounced and more mellow. It's up to you. Just be sure that you don't completely burn the sugar…it will smoke when it begins to burn and you'll have to throw it out, start again, and open all your windows. This recipe is unusual as it uses crème fraîche. If you don't have any on hand, replace it with an equal amount of whipping cream.

1 cup	200 g	sugar
2 Tbsp	30 mL	corn syrup
½ cup	125 mL	whipping cream
¼ cup	60 mL	crème fraîche
¼ tsp	1 mL	kosher salt
2 Tbsp	30 mL	butter (optional)
1 Tbsp	15 mL	Scotch (optional, but good!)

1. Place the sugar and corn syrup in a heavy, large saucepan over medium heat.

2. Stir with a wooden spoon until the sugar is dissolved. It will be sticky and lumpy at first. Break up the lumps with a wooden spoon and bring the mixture to a rolling boil. Place the lid on the pan for about 1 minute to allow the steam to dissolve any sugar crystals on the sides of the pan. Remove the lid.

3. For the first 10 minutes or so, you will have a lively, bubbling liquid. The bubbles will break with ease but gradually the mixture will thicken, the bubbles will start to slow down and you will hardly hear them bursting. Like an unruly child whose energy is spent, you will see the sugar subside to a quiet simmer. Eventually, the sugar will begin to darken in color.

4. Pay attention! The sugar caramelizes quickly now. Swirl the pan to distribute the caramelized sugar evenly. If it begins to darken too quickly, remove the pan from the heat.

5. When it reaches a rich, deep, golden brown, remove the pan from the heat and carefully add the whipping cream and crème fraîche, standing away from the pan to avoid being splattered and burned. The mixture will boil up furiously and produce prodigious amounts of steam. Keep your hands and face away from the volcanic action!

6. Return the pan to low heat and stir to dissolve any coagulated sugar. When completely smooth, remove from the heat and add the salt. (The French make a wonderful salted caramel. Try adding ½ tsp [2 mL] salt and notice how much more wonderful the caramel tastes!)

7. If you are making butterscotch sauce, add the butter and Scotch.

8. Let cool a bit before storing in a plastic container. This sauce has an indefinite shelf life and may be frozen. If it separates, just stir it back together. If it hardens, soften in a saucepan over low heat.

BROWNIE POINTS

Warm the sauce before using over ice cream and don't forget a sprinkling of salt on top. Simply out of this world.

Don't have much time? Dump all the ingredients into a heavy saucepan and bring to a boil over medium heat, stirring constantly. Boil for about 5 minutes. You won't get the same intensity of flavor but the sauce will be very, very good all the same.

chocolate fudge sauce

YIELD: 2 CUPS (500 mL)

My mother, Elaine, a fabulous impromptu cook, always used to make Baked Alaska for New Year's Eve, and everything was last minute, including the hot fudge sauce. She never used a recipe and as a result there were some years when the sauce was thick and flowing and other years when it congealed like lava over Pompeii, threatening a midnight rush to the dentist for a removed filling. Happily, that never happened, since we all learned to suck the pieces of hot fudge that we pried off the ice cream and the plate as if they were Tootsie Rolls. You shouldn't have that problem with this recipe unless you don't pay attention and boil it for too long.

4 oz	112 g	**unsweetened chocolate**
¼ cup	60 mL	**corn syrup**
1 cup	250 mL	**heavy cream**
½ cup	100 g	**granulated sugar**
½ cup	110 g	**brown sugar**
		pinch kosher salt

1. Place all the ingredients in a medium-sized heavy saucepan.
2. Bring to a boil over medium heat, stirring constantly until smooth.
3. Boil for 1 minute without stirring.
4. Remove from the heat and pour into a heatproof bowl to cool.
5. This stores indefinitely in the refrigerator or freezer in a tightly sealed container or squeeze bottle.
6. Reheat by putting it in a bowl over simmering water, or by putting the squeeze bottle (if you have stored it this way) directly into simmering water. Shake before using to make sure the entire contents have melted.

mixed salted nuts

YIELD: 3 CUPS (750 mL)

These are equally delicious as a cocktail nut or as a dessert embellishment. Make sure you buy your nuts from stores that have good turnover and avoid, if possible, walnuts from China, which tend to be unpleasantly bitter. Nuts are high in healthy oils but they burn easily, so keep an eye on them in the oven.

1 Tbsp	15 mL	kosher salt
3 cups	750 mL	water
2 tsp	10 mL	kosher salt, divided
2 tsp	10 mL	sugar, divided
3 oz	85 g	peanuts
3 oz	85 g	pecan halves
3 oz	85 g	hazelnuts, skinned
3 oz	85 g	walnut halves
3 oz	85 g	pine nuts

1. Bring the 1 Tbsp (15 mL) kosher salt and water to a boil in a medium saucepan.
2. Place ½ tsp (2 mL) of the remaining kosher salt and ½ tsp (2 mL) sugar in a medium-sized bowl and toss to mix.
3. Remove the pan from the heat.
4. Place the peanuts in a strainer that can be dipped into the boiling water just enough to moisten the nuts. Wet the peanuts and shake off any excess water.
5. Toss the peanuts with the salt and sugar mixture.
6. Spread the peanuts on a baking sheet.
7. Repeat steps 5 and 6 with the pecans, hazelnuts and walnuts.
8. Place the nuts in the oven. Toss once or twice while baking and bake until you can begin to smell their aromas, about 10–15 minutes. Do not let them overtoast. It is better to err on the side of underbrowning than overbrowning.
9. During the last 5 minutes, add the pine nuts.
10. Remove and cool completely. Store in a tightly sealed container, preferably in the freezer, for up to 2 months.

Hot 'n' spicy pecans

YIELD: 4 CUPS (1 L)

A company in Texas makes a really spicy version of these, but they're so expensive that I decided to make my own. They're easy and make great gifts, but they're also a wonderful addition to almost any brownie recipe, as you'll see! They can be stored, but not frozen, in an airtight container for about 2 months.

¼ cup	50 g	granulated sugar
½ tsp	2 mL	salt
1 tsp	5 mL	cinnamon
½ tsp	2 mL	ground ginger
½ tsp	2 mL	nutmeg, freshly ground
½ tsp	2 mL	ground coriander
½ tsp	2 mL	curry powder
¼ tsp	1 mL	cloves
¼ tsp	1 mL	cardamom
¼ tsp	1 mL	cayenne pepper
⅛ tsp	0.5 mL	allspice
2		egg whites
1 pound	454 g	pecan halves

1. Preheat the oven to 325°F (160°C). Line a baking sheet with parchment.

2. In a small bowl, mix together the sugar and all the spices.

3. In a medium bowl whisk the egg whites until they are frothy and loose.

4. Add the nuts and toss to coat.

5. Sprinkle the spiced sugar over the egg white-coated nuts and toss gently with a rubber spatula, making sure that the nuts are completely coated in the spice mixture.

6. Spread on the baking sheet.

7. Place in the oven and bake for a total of 30 minutes, stirring them at 10-minute intervals. After 20 minutes, reduce the temperature to 300°F (150°C) for the final 10 minutes.

8. Remove from the oven and cool completely. Break into individual pieces.

BROWNIE POINTS

Top off a Brownie Sundae with these nuts, whole or crumbled, for a great hot/sweet/salty/crunchy crowd pleaser.

Toss 1 cup (250 mL) of these into your favorite brownie recipe and bake as directed.

Toss into a salad.

RUMMED RAISINS

YIELD: 1 CUP (250 mL)

These are extraordinarily good and simple. Add them to your favorite brownie recipe, the Not So Wacky Brownie Cake (page 88) or the Ultimate, Ultimate Chocolate Chunk Cookies (page 103). Stored in a sealed jar in the fridge, they just get better and better.

1 cup	120 g	**dark or yellow raisins**
½ cup	125 mL	**good-quality rum**

1. Place the rum and raisins in a small saucepan and bring to a boil.
2. Shake the pan to coat the raisins completely.
3. Remove from the heat and let the raisins infuse with the rum.
4. Keep away from the kids!

BROWNIE CRUMBLE

YIELD: 2½ CUPS (675 mL)

There are several recipes for crunchy and chocolatey crumbles in this book. Try them all and see which you prefer.
I think they're all terrific and could eat them without anything underneath!

¼ cup	55 g	brown sugar
¾ cup	150 g	granulated sugar
¼ cup	30 g	cocoa
½ cup	65 g	all purpose flour
1 tsp	5 mL	baking soda
¼ tsp	1 mL	salt
4–8 Tbsp	60–125 mL	melted butter

1. Place both sugars, cocoa, flour, baking soda and salt in a mixing bowl.

2. Add half the butter and blend with your fingers to moisten the crumbs.

3. You should be able to squeeze the mixture in the palm of your hand and then sprinkle it between your fingers into pea-sized clumps. Add small amounts of the remaining butter as you mix. Don't add so much butter that it's like wet sand; nor should it be dry.

BROWNIE POINTS

Triple this recipe and freeze for future use. Throw it on cherries, strawberries or raspberries tossed with a little sugar, cornstarch and a squeeze of lemon juice for a quick crumble. Bake at 350°F (180°C) for about 30 minutes or until the fruit is bubbly and the crumble is firm. Dust with icing sugar before serving.

Spread raw crumble on a baking sheet and bake in a 300°F (150°C) oven for about 15–20 minutes or until firm. Cool. Sprinkle over ice cream or fruit salad for a snazzy garnish.

fabulously fudgy

Brownies

2

* The Fudge Factor indicates how comparitively moist and fudgy each brownie will be. See "Fudge Factor" on page 11.

first and foremost brownies

YIELD: 16 BARS

I love this recipe because it's fast and fudgy and provides a stable surrounding for so many of my favorite flavors: nuts, ginger and spices, to name just a few. The batter may be refrigerated or frozen almost indefinitely, so make twice the recipe. That way you'll always have some on hand for those pesky relatives or neighbors who keep turning up unexpectedly just to eat your famous brownies.

8 Tbsp	115 g	butter
8 oz	227 g	bittersweet chocolate
½ cup	110 g	brown sugar
½ cup	100 g	granulated sugar
3		eggs at room temperature
2 tsp	10 mL	vanilla extract
½ cup	65 g	all-purpose flour
¼ tsp	1 mL	kosher salt

1. Preheat the oven to 300°F (150°C). Line an 8- x 8-inch (20-x 20-cm) pan with overhanging parchment paper.

2. Melt the butter and cook until it becomes light brown and smells wonderful. Remove from the heat. Cool for 10 minutes.

3. Add the chocolate and melt. Stir until smooth.

4. Add the sugars and mix well. The mixture will be grainy.

5. Add the eggs one at a time, mixing until the batter is glossy and thick.

6. Add the vanilla, then the flour, mixing only enough to incorporate the flour.

7. Add the salt and mix briefly. (Adding the salt at the end of the mixing lends a wonderful contrast to the sweetness.)

8. Pour into the prepared pan and bake for 25–30 minutes. The edges will be firm but the center will be slightly soft, yet puffed. Remove from the oven and chill completely.

9. Slice into bars, wrap well and store in the fridge for up to a month, or in the freezer for up to 6 months.

elegant brownies

Make this simple shiny ganache and turn Basic Brownies into an easy, elegant dessert. Heat 1 cup (250 mL) cream to just below a boil. Place 10 oz. (280 g) of bittersweet chocolate, chopped, into a medium mixing bowl. Pour the hot cream over the chocolate. Add 1 Tbsp. (15 mL) corn syrup and let the mixture sit for about 10 minutes. Gently whisk the mixture until completely smooth, trying not to add any air in the form of bubbles. Use immediately or store in a covered container in the fridge for up to 2 weeks or freeze indefinitely. The best way to glaze the brownies is to chill them first. Turn the chilled slab upside down and remove the paper. Place the brownie slab on a baking rack set over a baking tray lined with parchment paper. Pour half the ganache in the center of the slab and spread it quickly to the sides, trying not to repeat your strokes over the chocolate more than once in order to maintain its smoothness and sheen. Let it set for about 2 hours before slicing. Place the brownie slab on a cutting board and slice into 16 bars, wiping the knife clean after every slice. To really gild the brownie, top each bar with a tiny piece of gold leaf.

tHe cLassic BROWNIe (aka my favorite BROWNIe)

YIELD: 6 CUPS (1.5 L) BATTER, OR 24 BARS IN A 9- x 13-INCH (23- x 33-CM) PAN

Everyone has a favorite brownie recipe and I'm no exception. My best food memory is coming home from school and entering the house to the incredible aroma of baking brownies. I could easily eat a pan myself but had the brakes put on me by my mom, who warned me about ruining my appetite before dinner. Somehow, even now, alas, that never happens…I always have an appetite, for dinner or any other meal, but especially for these brownies! Mom used the recipe on the back of the Baker's chocolate box, and to me these brownies are still among the best. Fudgy when not over-baked, a slight edge to them thanks to the bitter chocolate, and a depth of flavor I used to find unsurpassed until the world of gourmet chocolate arrived. These brownies are perfect as is, but they're even more decadent glazed with Ganache (page 28) or Shiny Chocolate Glaze (page 19). Be sure to read the Brownie Point before making the recipe!

1 cup	227 g	butter
1 cup	220 g	brown sugar
1 ½ cups	300 g	granulated sugar
12 oz	336 g	bittersweet chocolate, chopped
2 oz	56 g	unsweetened chocolate, chopped
6		eggs
1 Tbsp	15 mL	vanilla extract
1 tsp	5 mL	kosher salt
1 Tbsp	15 mL	instant coffee granules dissolved in 1 Tbsp (15 mL) hot water (optional)
1 cup	130 g	instant or all-purpose flour (see Brownie Point)

1. Preheat the oven to 300°F (150°C). Line a 9- x 13-inch (23- x 33-cm) pan with overhanging parchment paper.

2. In a medium saucepan, melt the butter over medium heat with the sugars. Use a heat-resistant spatula or a wire whisk to mix. At first, the liquefied butter will settle over the sugar. Keep stirring until the sugar and butter have completely combined. The sugar will still be somewhat granular, but it will have incorporated the butter into a single, smooth mass.

3. Remove from the heat and cool for 10 minutes. Add both chocolates. Whisk until smooth.

4. Add the eggs and whisk until the mixture is thick and shiny.

5. Add the vanilla, salt and optional dissolved coffee granules. Mix to blend.

6. Add the flour and whisk only until smooth.

7. Pour into the prepared pan.

8. Bake for 30–35 minutes only. The center will puff and the edges will appear glossy and firm. The center may appear soft underneath the surface, which is fine.

9. Remove from the oven and let cool to room temperature.

10. Refrigerate until firm.

11. Place a cutting board over the pan and turn upside down. Remove the parchment paper.

12. If you are glazing the brownies, do so bottom side up for an entirely smooth surface.

13. If you are eating them as is, invert them onto another board and slice into cubes, rectangles or triangles.

14. Store in the fridge wrapped in plastic for up to 2–3 weeks. Freeze wrapped in plastic and foil for up to 6 months.

BROWNIE POINT

The recipe makes almost 6 cups (1.5 L) of batter. Because many of my recipes call for this batter as an ingredient, you can make a smaller batch of brownies and freeze the rest of the batter. Pour the brownies into a parchment-lined 8- x 8-inch (20- x 20-cm) baking pan, ¾ of the way up the sides, and bake as instructed. Place the remaining batter in a freezer bag and refrigerate for up to 3 months or freeze indefinitely. Defrost before using.

Instant flour is found in the baking section of grocery stores as "Wondra."

GLUTEN-FREE CLASSIC BROWNIES

It seems that everyone is on some form of diet these days, depriving themselves of anything from fat to wheat, carbs or cholesterol. I have experimented with a lot of ingredients to replace some of what makes brownies nutritionally "naughty" and have had good success in many cases. This variation of Classic Brownies is a case in point. Substituting brown rice flour for wheat flour makes these entirely gluten-free, but they continue to provide a wallop of fudgy goodness. And, if it's only a few people who are wheat sensitive, you can easily adjust the recipe so that you prepare some Classic Brownies and some Gluten-free Classic Brownies with a minimum of additional effort.

Prepare the batter up to the addition of flour. Replace the wheat flour with 1 cup (140 g) of brown rice flour. Fill an 8- x 8-inch (20- x 20-cm) pan ¾ full with batter and bake as directed. Cool and chill completely before slicing. These are stickier than regular brownies and not quite as thick, but they're just as good!

BROWNIE TORTE

Turn a brownie into something elegant and easy...

1. Bake the brownies in a 9- x 13-inch (23- x 33-cm) baking pan.

2. When cool, slice lengthwise so you have two strips 4½ inches (12 cm) wide by 13 inches (33 cm) long.

3. Flavor 1 cup (250 mL) of Ganache (page 28) with 1 Tbsp (15 mL) strong coffee. Keep the glaze slightly warmer than room temperature, 80–85°F (27–30°C).

4. Toast 1 cup (120 g) pecan halves and cool. Chop fine in a food processor. Place the nut crumbs on a baking sheet.

5. Place one brownie strip, bottom side up, on a foil-wrapped piece of cardboard 4½ x 13 inches (12 x 33 cm) in the center of the platter. Set on a baking rack over a piece of parchment paper.

6. Pour ⅓ cup (80 mL) of glaze in the center of the cake. Using a spatula, gently coax the glaze to the edges. Let it sit and cool for 5–10 minutes.

7. Place the second brownie strip over the first, bottom side up.

8. Pour the remaining glaze over the top and spread evenly to the sides, pushing it gently over the edges and down the sides. Quickly spread the glaze on all four sides.

9. Lift the torte over the tray with the chopped nuts. Scoop up the nuts and gently pat them onto the sides of the cake from the bottom up, to create an even band of nuts around the cake. Work quickly because, as the glaze sets, it won't hold the crumbs.

10. Let the cake set for about 15 minutes before serving. Or, store in the fridge up to 3 days.

11. Serve slices on a pool of Crème Anglaise (page 27) and garnish with fresh raspberries.

Balsamic Brownies

YIELD: 16 BARS

Inspiration strikes in strange ways. Frequently I'll open my kitchen cabinets and root around the savory ingredients to see if there's something exotic that might go fabulously with chocolate. Recently, there were great strawberries at Whole Foods Market, where I work. Simultaneously, balsamic vinegar was on special so I bought some to sprinkle on my strawberries, a classic Italian combination. Suddenly it occurred to me: if strawberries go well with balsamic vinegar, and strawberries go well with chocolate, doesn't logic tell me that the balsamic vinegar and chocolate ought to go well together? It was a stretch, to be sure, but just wait until you taste these brownies. And, following my logic, these go beautifully with a sauce of crushed and slightly sweetened strawberries!

13 Tbsp	185 g	butter, cubed
2 ½ oz	70 g	white chocolate, chopped
4 oz	112 g	unsweetened chocolate, chopped
2 Tbsp	30 mL	cocoa
2 cups	400 g	sugar
2 Tbsp	30 mL	balsamic vinegar
½ tsp	2 mL	kosher salt
5		eggs, lightly beaten
¼ cup	35 g	all-purpose flour

1. Preheat the oven to 300°F (150°C). Grease a 9- x 9-inch (23- x 23-cm) pan. Line with overhanging parchment paper.

2. Place the butter in a microwave-safe 2-cup (500-mL) measure and melt on high power for approximately 45 seconds.

3. Place both chocolates in the bowl of a food processor and process until reduced to a fine powder.

4. Add the cocoa and sugar and process to combine.

5. Add the balsamic vinegar and salt to the melted butter. With the motor running, pour the mixture through the feed tube and process until smooth. Stop, scrape the sides of the bowl and pulse to blend thoroughly.

6. With the motor running, gradually pour in the eggs. Mix until smooth.

7. Add the flour and pulse until completely absorbed.

8. Pour into the prepared pan and bake for 30 minutes, until slightly puffed in the center.

9. Cool completely before slicing.

Blood orange balsamic brownies

YIELD: **16** BARS

One day, blood oranges caught my eye in the produce department at Whole Foods Market. A tart orange with an intense flavor, I thought it would make a nice foil to the sweet richness of Balsamic Brownies (previous page). This is a real showstopper.

10 Tbsp	140 g	**butter**
7 oz	195 g	**white chocolate, chopped**
3 oz	90 g	**unsweetened chocolate, chopped**
2 ½ Tbsp	20 g	**cocoa**
1 ½ cups less 1 Tbsp	260 g	**sugar**
¼ tsp	1 mL	**kosher salt**
2		**blood oranges, zest grated**
1 Tbsp + 2 tsp	25 mL	**balsamic vinegar**
3 Tbsp + 1 tsp	50 mL	**blood orange juice**
4		**eggs**
¼ cup	35 g	**all-purpose flour**

1. Preheat the oven to 300°F (150°C). Line 9- x 9-inch (23- x 23-cm) pan with overhanging parchment paper.

2. Place the butter in a microwave-safe 2-cup (500-mL) measure. Place in the microwave and melt on high power for about 1 minute.

3. In the bowl of a food processor fitted with the steel blade, place both chocolates, cocoa, sugar and salt. Process until powdery.

4. Add the grated orange zest.

5. Whisk together the vinegar, orange juice and eggs in a separate bowl.

6. With the processor running, add the melted butter and white chocolate through the feed tube. Scrape down the sides. With the machine running, pour in the egg mixture and pulse to blend thoroughly.

7. Add the flour and blend briefly until smooth.

8. Pour into the prepared pan and bake for 30 minutes or until just set. Cool completely before removing from the pan.

brownie point

These are extremely good served warm with a cool contrast, like sweetened, whipped, mascarpone cheese or crème fraîche.

banana coconut ginger brownies

YIELD: 16 BARS

We all have our culinary disasters. The first time I made these, they puffed up like a foam pillow and had the texture to match, as recipes with bananas have a tendency to do. However, the combination of chocolate and bananas is a favorite of mine, so I reworked the recipe and voila!

1 cup less 1 Tbsp	212 g	**butter**
¼ cup	30 g	**cocoa, sifted**
¾ cup less 1 Tbsp	150 g	**brown sugar**
¾ cup	150 g	**granulated sugar**
2		**eggs**
8 oz	227 g	**bittersweet chocolate, melted**
3 ½ oz	100 g	**white chocolate, melted**
1 Tbsp	15 mL	**rum**
2		**ripe medium bananas, peeled and mashed**
2 Tbsp	30 mL	**sour cream**
1 Tbsp	15 mL	**finely grated fresh ginger**
½ cup	50 g	**toasted coconut**
½ cup	65 g	**all-purpose flour**

1. Preheat the oven to 300°F (150°C). Line a 9- x 9-inch (23- x 23-cm) pan with overhanging parchment paper.

2. Melt the butter and add the cocoa. Mix to blend thoroughly.

3. Add both sugars. Stir until smooth.

4. Add the eggs one at a time and mix well.

5. Add both chocolates and mix until shiny and smooth.

6. Add the rum, bananas, sour cream, ginger and coconut. Mix to incorporate.

7. Add the flour and mix only to blend.

8. Pour into the prepared pan and bake for 30 minutes.

9. Remove and cool completely before cutting.

BROWNIE POINT

To make these more glamorous, glaze with Ganache (page 28) and sprinkle toasted, long-shred coconut on top. Let set before slicing with a hot knife, washed and wiped dry between each slice.

Bar None Brownies

YIELD: 16 BARS

These are gooey, nutty and emit an absolutely heavenly aroma while baking. In this case, I don't stint on the kind of chocolate I use, going for only the best: Scharffen Berger Bitter Chocolate and a good quality bittersweet to complement it. While you can use other chocolates, none will provide the depth of flavor and mouth-feel, as we say in the industry, as Scharffen Berger.

1 cup	227 g	butter
7 oz	195 g	Scharffen Berger bitter chocolate
3 oz	85 g	good quality bittersweet chocolate
4		eggs
2 cups	220 g	brown sugar
1 Tbsp	15 mL	strong coffee
1 Tbsp	15 mL	vanilla extract
1 cup	130 g	all-purpose flour
¾ tsp	4 mL	baking powder
1 tsp	5 mL	kosher salt, divided
9 oz	250 g	milk chocolate, coarsely chopped
6 oz	250 g	toasted pecans, coarsely chopped

1. Preheat the oven to 300°F (150°C). Line a 9- x 9-inch (23- x 23-cm) pan with overhanging parchment paper.

2. In a medium saucepan, melt the butter and the bitter and bittersweet chocolates over low heat. Mix with a rubber spatula until smooth. Remove from the heat and let cool.

3. Meanwhile, place the eggs and sugar in the bowl of an electric mixer.

4. Beat on medium speed until it's light and fluffy and has tripled in volume, about 10 minutes.

5. Gradually pour the chocolate mixture into the egg mixture, beating on low speed until completely incorporated. (By this time, you will be intoxicated by the wonderful aroma.) Mix in the coffee and vanilla.

6. Mix the flour, baking powder and half the salt.

7. Add the flour gradually to the chocolate batter and mix for about 1 minute. Remove the bowl from the mixer, scrape the batter from the beaters and use a rubber spatula to gently scrape the sides and bottom of the bowl. Mix until the batter is completely combined.

8. Add the milk chocolate and pecans. Blend gently.

9. Pour into the pan and spread evenly. Crush the remaining ½ tsp (2 mL) kosher salt between your fingers while sprinkling it evenly on top of the batter.

10. Bake for about 35–40 minutes. The center will still test gooey with a toothpick but will firm up in the fridge. Don't over bake.

11. While these are sensational any way you eat them, they are by far the best when served warm with vanilla ice cream and eaten at midnight.

Brownie Point

If you want these to be a bit more chi-chi, double the amount of toasted pecans and chop half, keeping the rest whole. Mix the chopped pieces into the batter and smooth the top. Place the whole pecan pieces, rounded side down, into the batter and bake. Let cool completely and drizzle warmed Ganache (page 28) over the top. Cool completely before slicing.

CHOCOLATE RASPBERRY PEANUT BUTTER CRUMBLE BARS

YIELD: 24 BARS

Some people fantasize about sex; me, I fantasize about brownies (sorry, Howard) and how I can pack just about every flavor and texture I love into a single bar. These come pretty close to perfection, what with creamy peanut butter, rich, fudgy chocolate, the tang of raspberries and the crunch of crumble. Okay, so it's no substitute for sex, but it comes pretty close!

1 pint	150 g	raspberries
1 Tbsp	15 mL	sugar
2 ¾ cups	360 g	all-purpose flour
¼ cup	30 g	cocoa
1 ½ tsp	7 mL	baking soda
1 ½ tsp	7 mL	baking powder
½ tsp	2 mL	kosher salt
1 cup	227 g	butter
1 cup	250 mL	peanut butter
1 cup + 2 Tbsp	225 g	sugar
2		eggs
2 tsp	10 mL	vanilla extract
1 cup	175 g	chocolate chips
½ cup	125 mL	Ganache (page 28)
		icing sugar for dusting

1. Preheat the oven to 350°F (180°C). Grease a 9- x13-inch (23- x 33-cm) baking pan and line with overhanging parchment paper.

2. In a small saucepan, heat the raspberries and 1 Tbsp (15 mL) sugar until the raspberries become soft. Remove from the heat and cool.

3. Mix together the flour, cocoa, baking soda, baking powder and salt. Set aside. This is your raspberry purée.

4. In the bowl of an electric mixer, beat the butter and peanut butter together until smooth.

5. Add the sugar and beat until mixed, scraping the sides from time to time, about 2 minutes.

6. Add the eggs one at a time, scraping the sides of the bowl after each addition.

7. Add the vanilla and blend briefly.

8. Add the flour and cocoa mixture and mix only until blended.

9. Remove 1½ cups (375 mL) of batter from the bowl and place in a second bowl. Add the chocolate chips to the bowl and mix with a rubber spatula.

10. Press the batter without the chocolate chips into the prepared pan. Spread the raspberry purée on top.

11. Create a crumble topping by dropping the batter with the chocolate chips in little blobs evenly over the surface of the raspberry purée.

12. Bake for about 25–30 minutes, watching carefully that the crumble doesn't burn.

13. Remove from the oven and cool completely.

14. Drizzle with ganache and let set.

15. Dust with icing sugar and slice.

fudgy BROWNIE CHRISTMAS PUDDING   p. 126

fresh fruit chocolate crumble p. 144

INCREDIBLE PEAR HAZELNUT TART p. 148

chunky pecan milk chocolate brownies

YIELD: 24 BARS

I wish I could say that inspiration is always a eureka moment. All too often, a recipe such as this one evolves due to my frugal nature: I would rather use up odds and sods of ingredients than throw them out. In this case, it was exactly 60 g, or about ½ cup, of toasted pecans sitting on my counter for weeks and weeks that forced inspiration. Why I didn't just put them in the freezer, where I could have forgotten about them altogether, I don't know. Happily though, this delectable recipe was the result.

1 cup	227 g	**butter**
7 oz	200 g	**unsweetened chocolate**
3 oz	85 g	**bittersweet chocolate**
2 cups	440 g	**brown sugar**
4		**eggs**
1 Tbsp	15 mL	**strong coffee**
1 tsp	5 mL	**vanilla extract**
1 tsp	5 mL	**kosher salt**
1 cup	130 g	**all-purpose flour**
¾ tsp	4 mL	**baking powder**
6 oz	170 g	**milk chocolate, coarsely chopped**
1 ½ cups	150 g	**pecans, coarsely chopped**

1. Preheat the oven to 350°F (180°C). Line a 9- x 13-inch (23- x 33-cm) pan with overhanging parchment paper.

2. Melt the butter in a medium saucepan over medium heat. Add the unsweetened and bittersweet chocolate and stir until completely melted and blended.

3. Remove from the heat and blend in the brown sugar.

4. Add the eggs one at a time, mixing thoroughly until the batter is thick and glossy.

5. Mix in the coffee, vanilla and salt.

6. Mix the flour with the baking powder and stir into the batter, mixing only enough to incorporate the flour.

7. Stir in the milk chocolate chunks and chopped pecans.

8. Pour into the prepared pan and bake for 30 minutes. Cool before slicing.

cocoa brownies

YIELD: **16** BARS

In our bakery/restaurant, The Original Bakery Café, we started with a brownie recipe that required melting more than 20 pounds (10 kg) of chocolate. Because it was good chocolate, it also had to be chopped. The task was dreaded by everyone who had their name next to the brownies on the prep list. As a result, we developed a cocoa brownie recipe that combined the best aspects of both recipes: dense and fudgy, but without the fuss. In this recipe, I brown the butter for a greater depth of flavor. Be sure to allow the butter to cool a bit before adding the cocoa.

1½ cups	340 g	**butter**
½ cup	60 g	**cocoa**
1½ cups	300 g	**sugar**
4		**eggs**
1 Tbsp	15 mL	**vanilla extract**
1 Tbsp	15 mL	**strong coffee**
⅔ cup	85 g	**all-purpose flour**
½ tsp	2 mL	**kosher salt**

1. Preheat the oven to 300°F (150°C). Line a 9- x 9-inch (23- x 23-cm) pan with overhanging parchment paper.

2. In a medium saucepan, melt the butter over medium heat until it bubbles and browns. It will froth and then settle down, with the milk solids settling to the bottom. Be sure not to burn the butter.

3. Remove from the heat, cool slightly and add the cocoa. Whisk until smooth.

4. Add the sugar and whisk until smooth. Cool for 10 minutes.

5. Add the eggs, whisking until smooth and shiny.

6. Blend in the vanilla and coffee.

7. Add the flour and salt, whisking only until blended.

8. Pour into the prepared pan and bake for 30 minutes.

9. Allow to cool, then refrigerate.

10. Remove from the pan by inverting onto a rack and then again onto a cutting board. Cut them as big or small as you like.

11. Store well wrapped in plastic and foil in the fridge for up to 2 weeks, and in the freezer for up to 6 months.

coffee toffee BARS OR BROWNIES

YIELD: 24 BARS, OR 12 BARS AND 16 BROWNIES

Can't decide if you want brownies or not? Then these bars are for you! Two recipes in one, together they make a gangbuster treat! You'll need Classic Brownie batter to make the complete recipe, so plan ahead.

1 cup	227 g	butter, softened
2 cups	440 g	brown sugar
1 Tbsp	15 mL	vanilla extract
1 Tbsp	15 mL	instant coffee granules dissolved in 1 Tbsp (15 mL) hot water
3		eggs
1 ½ cups	200 g	all-purpose flour
½ tsp	2 mL	salt
8 oz	225 g	toffee chips
4 oz	115 g	pecans, toasted and chopped
3 cups	750 mL	Classic Brownie batter (page 42)
½ cup	125 mL	Ganache (page 28)

1. Preheat the oven to 300°F (150°C). Line a 9- x 13-inch (23- x 33-cm) pan with overhanging parchment paper.

2. Place the butter and sugar in the bowl of an electric mixer fitted with the paddle attachment. Beat on medium speed until smooth, about 3 minutes, scraping the sides and bottom occasionally.

3. Add the vanilla and instant coffee dissolved in hot water. Beat until smooth.

4. Add the eggs one at a time, scraping the sides and bottom of the bowl after each addition.

5. Add the flour and salt, mixing just enough to incorporate fully.

6. Remove the bowl from the mixer and gently fold in the toffee chips and pecans.

7. Spread the batter into the prepared pan.

8. Bake for about 30 minutes or until slightly puffy but not fully set in the center. It should be a little soft but not raw. Since there's no chocolate in this batter, it won't firm up in the fridge quite as much, but that's okay because it's delicious anyway!

9. Allow to cool before removing from the pan. (At this point you can eat all the bars as is or continue with the recipe,…I vote to continue!)

10. When completely cool (it's better if it has been refrigerated) break half the slab into chunky pieces about the size of a whole walnut.

11. Gently fold the pieces into the Classic Brownie batter.

12. Spread the batter in a 9- x 9-inch (23- x 23-cm) brownie pan lined with overhanging parchment paper.

13. Bake at 300°F (150°C) for 30 minutes, not a minute more.

14. Cool, then drizzle with warmed Ganache.

15. Lift out, cut and serve!

CRUISE SHIP BROWNIES

YIELD: 24 BARS

Knowing I was writing a brownie book, my ever-vigilant parents requested and received this recipe from the chef of a large cruise ship. It's delicious and has been downsized from its original, which called for 2 pounds (1 kg) of chocolate, 5 pounds (2.5 kg) of butter, 12 cups (2.4 kg) of sugar and 32 eggs! I have altered the technique for a fudgier result.

⅔ cup	150 g	butter
5 ½ oz	150 g	bittersweet chocolate, chopped
1 ¼ cups	250 g	sugar
4		eggs
1 cup	130 g	all-purpose flour
½ tsp	2 mL	baking powder
¼ tsp	1 mL	salt
5 ½ oz	150 g	bittersweet chocolate, chopped
5 ½ oz	150 g	walnuts, toasted

1. Preheat the oven to 300°F (150°C). Line an 8- x 8-inch (20- x 20-cm) pan with overhanging parchment paper.

2. In a medium saucepan, melt the butter.

3. Add the first 5½ oz (150 g) of chocolate to the pan and return to low heat, stirring as it melts, until the mixture is completely smooth. Remove from the heat and cool 5 minutes.

4. Add the sugar. The mixture will be thick

5. Add the eggs and mix until the batter is thick and glossy.

6. Add the flour, baking powder and salt, and mix until just blended.

7. Add the remaining chopped chocolate and the toasted nuts. Mix thoroughly to incorporate. (One half cup Rummed Raisins [page 37] would be good too!)

8. Pour into the prepared pan, spread evenly and bake for 30 minutes.

9. Remove and cool. The brownies will be rich and dense!

BROWNIE POINT

Turn this into an elegant Brownie Pie: pour the batter into a 9-inch (23-cm) glass pie dish and evenly dot the top with whole pecans placed flat side up. Bake in a 300°F (150°C) oven for about 40 minutes or until the center is wet but firm. Cool for about 30 minutes before serving. It will be crisp around the edges and gooey in the center. Pass around some vanilla ice cream and Caramel Butterscotch Sauce (page 32).

extreme BROWNIes

YIELD: TWO 12- X 15-INCH (30- X 38-CM) PANS OR THREE 9- X 13-INCH (23- X 33-CM) PANS

You've heard of Extreme Sports – those on-the-edge, daring activities that most of us watch on TV while happily downing brownies and milk. Here's a brownie version, loaded with Rummed Raisins and cocoa nibs (tiny pieces of unprocessed cocoa beans that add crunch and a slight bitterness to every bite), not to mention pecans and chocolate chips. If you want them thin, bake them in the two larger pans, but if, like me, you like something substantial, divide the batter among three smaller pans for thicker bars.

1 pound	454 g	butter, divided
6½ oz	185 g	70% bittersweet chocolate
1 pound	454 g	bittersweet chocolate
6		eggs
1 cup	200 g	granulated sugar
½ cup	110 g	dark brown or muscovado sugar
2 Tbsp	30 mL	vanilla extract
1½ cups	210 g	whole wheat flour
1 Tbsp	15 mL	baking powder
1 tsp	5 mL	kosher salt
1½ cups	375 mL	Rummed Raisins (page 37)
8 oz	227 g	pecans, toasted and cooled
1 cup	115 g	cocoa nibs

BROWNIE POINT

Cocoa nibs are available at gourmet stores or on the Web from the wonderful people at Scharffen Berger Chocolate in San Francisco. While you're at it, get some of their unsweetened and 70% chocolate. I think it's the best there is for baking. You can contact them at www.scharffenberger.com for more information.

1. Preheat the oven to 300°F (150°C). Line the pans with overhanging parchment paper.

2. Place half the butter in a large saucepan and melt slowly over low heat.

3. Add the two chocolates when the butter is half melted. Stir occasionally to make sure the chocolate doesn't stick to the bottom and burn.

4. When the chocolate is almost completely melted, turn off the heat. Add the remaining butter, which will melt and cool the chocolates.

5. Meanwhile, stir the eggs gently with the granulated and brown sugars until blended. Add the vanilla and blend.

6. Pour the melted, cooled chocolate into a large bowl. Gradually add the sugar and eggs, stirring quickly to blend thoroughly. The mixture will be thick and glossy with an ethereal aroma. Don't get waylaid by wanting to drink it! Keep going!

7. Mix the flour with the baking powder and salt.

8. Gradually add the dry ingredients to the chocolate mixture, mixing gently but thoroughly to make a completely smooth batter.

9. Add the Rummed Raisins and any accumulated juices, along with the nuts and cocoa nibs. Mix to blend.

10. Divide the batter among the prepared pans and bake for 30 minutes, not a minute more! The top should not puff up or dome. The edges will be firm but the center will still be soft without being liquid.

11. Cool completely. Cut with a sharp, wet knife, wiping the knife between cuts. The bars may be frozen, well-wrapped in plastic and foil, for up to 6 months (and probably a lot longer!), or stored in the fridge, wrapped the same way, for weeks and weeks.

five nuts in a pan brownies

YIELD: 16 BARS

This recipe is an ode to everyone who loves chocolate and nuts, and to those who are simply nuts over chocolate! These are amazing brownies with a shiny surface glistening with caramel sauce bubbling over with nuts. Serve warm with vanilla or ginger ice cream and you'll be in seventh heaven.

2 oz	56 g	**coarsely chopped pecans**
2 oz	56 g	**almonds, in any form**
2 oz	56 g	**whole, peeled hazelnuts**
2 oz	56 g	**walnut pieces**
2 oz	56 g	**pine nuts**
4 cups	1 L	**Classic Brownie batter (page 42)**
1 cup	250 mL	**Caramel Butterscotch Sauce (page 32)**

1. Preheat the oven to 300°F (150°C). Line a 9- x 9-inch (23- x 23-cm) pan with overhanging parchment paper.

2. Place all the nuts on a baking tray and bake in the oven for 10 minutes, stirring occasionally. Remove from the oven and cool. Place in a medium-sized bowl.

3. Spread the brownie batter evenly in the prepared pan. Place in the oven and bake for 25 minutes.

4. Five minutes before the brownies are ready, heat the Caramel Sauce in the microwave until it is warm and liquid, about 1 ½ minutes. Pour the sauce over the nuts and mix gently to coat.

5. Remove the brownies from the oven and drop the nut mixture over the brownies using a soup spoon. Spread them gently in an even layer, using an offset spatula. Don't press too hard or the nuts will go into the brownies. If they go in a bit, don't worry about it. You just don't want them to be submerged.

6. Return the pan to the oven for an additional 5–7 minutes, or until the sauce starts to bubble around the edges. Don't allow it to bake too much, since it can quickly go from golden to burned.

7. Remove the brownies from the oven and cool to room temperature. Loosen the brownie slab by running a spatula around the edges before trying to remove it from the pan. Cool completely.

8. Using the overhanging parchment paper, lift the brownie slab out of the pan and admire your handiwork!

9. These brownies are best cut with a heavy chef's knife that is slightly wet. Wipe the blade clean after each slice to achieve a neat edge and a professional look.

BROWNIE POINT

There are a number of techniques to remove the skin from hazelnuts, most of them really annoying. Recently, however, I discovered a new quick and easy way. Place the hazelnuts on a microwavable plate and cook on high power for about 1 ½ minutes. Remove and place the nuts in a clean dishtowel. Rub the nuts between your hands and the skin flakes off. For those nuts that insist on keeping their skin, just put them back in the microwave for another minute or so.

fLourLess BROWNies

YIELD: 16 BARS

The Jewish holiday of Passover always poses baking challenges. No ordinary flour and absolutely no leavening agents, such as baking powder, soda or yeast, are allowed. Hence there are dozens of recipes for egg-leavened tortes, chiffon, and jelly-roll-type cakes. Most of these are what I would characterize as traditional cakes and don't elicit the oohs and aahs that spur contemporary bakers to create new and amazing recipes. So every Passover, I set out to create the most chocolatey flourless dessert possible. This is one of them. You certainly don't have to wait for Passover to serve these brownies and they're perfect for anyone with a gluten allergy.

2 oz	56 g	unsweetened chocolate, chopped
4 oz	112 g	bittersweet chocolate, chopped
1 cup	227 g	butter, in cubes
1 cup	200 g	sugar
1 Tbsp	15 mL	cocoa
1 Tbsp	15 mL	molasses
¾ tsp	4 mL	kosher salt
4		eggs, lightly beaten
4 oz	112 g	pecans, toasted and finely ground
4 oz	112 g	whole pecan pieces, toasted

1. Preheat the oven to 300°F (150°C). Grease an 8- x 8-inch (20- x 20-cm) pan and line with overhanging parchment paper.

2. Place both chocolates and the butter, sugar, cocoa, molasses and salt in a medium saucepan over low heat.

3. Stir until the chocolate and butter are melted and the sugar, cocoa, and molasses are thoroughly blended. It's okay if the mixture is grainy with sugar.

4. Remove the pan from the heat and whisk in the eggs. The batter will be thick and glossy.

5. Add the ground nuts and stir well.

6. Pour the batter into the prepared pan. Top with an even layer of whole pecans.

7. Bake for 30 minutes or until the edges are firm but the center is still jiggly.

8. Cool to room temperature and then refrigerate.

9. These brownies are incredible when still slightly warm, unstoppable when room temperature, and densely chewy and delicious when cold. They also last forever.

10. Cut into small pieces because they are rich!

BROWNie POINt

Toasted ground and whole almonds and ½ tsp (2 mL) of almond extract are a delicious substitute for the pecans.

ganache brownies

YIELD: 16 BARS

I developed this recipe, like so many others, because I had some excess ganache sitting in the fridge. Doesn't everyone have this problem?

1¼ cups	310 mL	**Ganache (page 28), divided**
2 Tbsp	30 mL	**butter**
2		**eggs**
¼ tsp	1 mL	**salt**
1 tsp	5 mL	**instant coffee granules dissolved in 1 Tbsp (15 mL) hot water**
		pinch cinnamon
¼ cup	35 g	**all-purpose flour**
5 oz	150 g	**whole pecans**
¾ cup	175 mL	**Caramel Butterscotch Sauce (page 32)**
		pinch sea salt

1. Preheat the oven to 300°F (150°C). Line a 9- x 9-inch (23- x 23-cm) pan with overhanging parchment paper.

2. Place 1 cup (250 mL) of the ganache in a bowl and set over a pot of simmering water.

3. Stir until melted. Remove the bowl from the pot.

4. Add the butter, eggs, salt, coffee and cinnamon, mixing until smooth.

5. Add the flour and mix just until thoroughly incorporated.

6. Pour into the prepared pan and bake for 30 minutes. Remove from the oven and spread the pecans over the top.

7. Drizzle Caramel Butterscotch Sauce over the pecans and return to the oven until just bubbly, about 5 minutes.

8. Remove from the oven and lightly sprinkle fine sea salt over the caramel.

9. Cool. Warm the remaining ¼ cup (60 mL) Ganache and drizzle over the brownie slab. Let the Ganache set.

10. Lift the slab out of the pan using the parchment paper. Use a chef's knife and a firm slicing motion to achieve perfect edges. And don't forget to wipe your knife after every cut!

GROWN UP ROCKY ROAD BROWNIES

YIELD: 16 BARS

"Rocky Road" is usually an excuse for adding just about everything to a dish, which usually ends up being extremely sweet (look who's talking!). The rum-soaked raisins, however, mean this recipe is definitely for adults and not nearly as sweet as its various namesakes.

7 Tbsp	100 g	**butter**
4 oz	112 g	**unsweetened chocolate**
4 oz	112 g	**milk chocolate**
¾ cup	165 g	**brown sugar**
1 Tbsp	15 mL	**molasses**
3		**eggs**
¼ cup	35 g	**all-purpose flour**
½ tsp	2 mL	**kosher salt**
¾ cup	175 mL	**Rummed Raisins (page 37)**
1 cup	80 g	**mini marshmallows, divided**
3 oz	85 g	**walnuts, toasted and coarsely chopped**

1. Preheat the oven to 300°F (150°C). Line a 9- x 9-inch (23- x 23-cm) pan with overhanging parchment paper.

2. In a heavy saucepan melt the butter and both chocolates over low heat. Whisk until smooth.

3. Blend in the sugar and molasses.

4. Add the eggs and whisk until smooth.

5. Add the flour and salt and whisk until blended.

6. Add the raisins and half the marshmallows. Fold them in gently.

7. Pour into the prepared pan and spread until even.

8. Spread the remaining marshmallows over the top and place the walnuts in between the marshmallows to completely cover the top.

9. Bake for 35 minutes. Let cool before lifting out of the pan.

Golden coconut brownies

YIELD: 16 BARS

As with many of my recipes, these brownies will stand up just fine on their own without the topping. However, if you double the macaroon recipe, you can use half to make flourless macaroons (see Brownie Point). Once assembled, the macaroon batter may be kept in the fridge and scooped and baked to order over the course of about a week.

BROWNIE Batter:

8 Tbsp	115 g	**butter**
1 ½ oz	42 g	**unsweetened chocolate**
1 ½ oz	42 g	**bittersweet chocolate**
¾ cup	100 g	**instant or all-purpose flour** (see Brownie Point on page 42)
¼ tsp	1 mL	**kosher salt**
¼ tsp	1 mL	**baking powder**
3		**eggs**
½ cup	100 g	**granulated sugar**
½ cup	110 g	**brown sugar**
½ Tbsp	8 mL	**vanilla extract**
1 recipe		**Macaroon Topping**

1. Preheat the oven to 300°F (150°C). Line an 8- x 8-inch (20- x 20-cm) pan with overhanging parchment paper.

2. Place the butter and both chocolates in a medium saucepan and set over low heat. Whisk frequently to make sure the chocolate doesn't burn. Remove the pan from the heat before the butter and chocolate have melted completely, allowing the residual heat to do the rest of the work. Whisk to make the mixture smooth.

3. In a small bowl, mix together the flour, salt and baking powder. Set aside.

4. In the bowl of an electric mixer fitted with the whisk attachment, whisk the eggs, both sugars and the vanilla until triple in volume, about 5 minutes.

5. With the mixer on low speed, pour in the melted chocolate.

6. Scrape the bottom and sides of the bowl.

7. Add the dry ingredients and mix only enough to incorporate thoroughly.

8. Pour into the prepared pan and smooth the top.

9. If you are not baking immediately, place the brownies in the fridge.

10. Otherwise, spread the Macaroon Topping over the brownie batter in the pan.

11. Bake until the macaroon topping is golden, about 30 minutes (add an extra 5 minutes if the brownies have been refrigerated). Cool in the fridge before cutting.

macaroon topping:

2		egg whites
½ cup	100 g	sugar
2 cups	200 g	sweetened, long shred coconut
½ tsp	2 mL	vanilla extract
¼ tsp	1 mL	kosher salt

1. Place the egg whites and sugar in a large saucepan set over low-medium heat.

2. Use a whisk to stir constantly. You don't want the eggs to sit and cook!

3. The sugar will dissolve and you will see bubbles on the surface. From time to time, dip your pinky finger into the batter. You want it to be hot but no hotter than 140°F (70°C). Tepid is too cool and if it is really hot, it will turn into scrambled eggs, so keep an eye on it. To be sure, use an instant read thermometer to guide you.

4. When it is hot, remove the pan from the heat and stir in the coconut. Return the pan to the heat and stir constantly on low heat for another 5 minutes. The mixture will thicken considerably.

5. Remove it from the heat and stir in the vanilla and salt.

BROWNIE POINT

Double the topping recipe and use half to make macaroons. Scoop tablespoon-sized blobs onto a cookie sheet lined with parchment paper. Press the balls with the palm of your hand to flatten them, and bake at 300°F (150°C) until golden brown on the outside. They may still be soft on the inside but they will continue to cook when removed from the oven. If you overbake them, they will be deliciously crispy, but their shelf-life will be greatly reduced because you have baked away much of the moisture. Store in an airtight container to maintain chewiness.

ᴊᴄᴋSON PoLLock Bars

YIELD: 20 BARS

I love the traditional 7-layer bars, sometimes known as Congo bars, but as I get older, they've become too sweet for my taste. Here's my adult version with a finish that makes them look just like a Jackson Pollock canvas. You need Classic Brownie batter, Ganache and Caramel Butterscotch Sauce to complete them quickly.

8 Tbsp	115 g	**butter**
3 cups	750 mL	**graham cracker crumbs**
3 oz	85 g	**whole hazelnuts, toasted and peeled**
3 oz	85 g	**hazelnuts , peeled, toasted and chopped**
1 cup	100 g	**toasted coconut**
1 cup	250 mL	**Classic Brownie batter (page 42)**
1 cup	250 mL	**sweetened condensed milk**
2 Tbsp	30 mL	**finely chopped candied ginger**
2 ½ oz	75 g	**slivered almonds**
¼ cup	60 mL	**Ganache (page 28)**
¼ cup	60 mL	**Caramel Butterscotch Sauce (page 32)**

1. Preheat the oven to 300°F (150°C). Line a 9- x 13-inch (23- x 33-cm) pan with overhanging parchment paper.

2. Place the butter in a small saucepan over low heat and melt until it has turned a golden brown.

3. Mix with the graham cracker crumbs and press into the bottom of the prepared pan. It will be a fairly thin layer.

4. Bake in the oven for 15 minutes.

5. Remove from the oven and sprinkle with the whole hazelnuts, then the chopped hazelnuts on top.

6. Sprinkle the toasted coconut over the hazelnuts.

7. Mix the brownie batter with the sweetened condensed milk and drizzle over the coconut.

8. Distribute the ginger and the slivered almonds evenly on top.

9. Bake for about 25 minutes or until slightly bubbly on top. Don't overbake.

10. Remove from the oven and cool completely.

11. Warm both the ganache and the caramel sauce to the point where they are just pourable, about 80–85°F (27–30°C).

12. From a height of about 2 feet (60 cm), evenly drizzle first the ganache and then the caramel over the top to create a splattered, drizzled effect.

13. Let firm up before slicing into bars.

sugarless (date) brownies

YIELD: 24 BARS

When I wrote the proposal for this book, I swore there would be no low-fat, low-sugar, i.e., fad diet, recipes. But when I came upon some Medjool dates and bought an entire case, it occurred to me that maybe, just maybe, I could come up with an oft-requested item: a sweet without refined sugar. Medjool dates are incredibly sweet and succulent but need to be softened. I tried wine and white grape juice, eventually settling on plain water and some honey for added sweetness. These bars are soft and dense, not quite fudgy and not too sweet, which is a nice change every now and then.

12		Medjool dates, pits removed
1 cup less 1 Tbsp	235 mL	water
3 Tbsp	45 mL	honey
5 oz	140 g	unsweetened chocolate, chopped
6 Tbsp	85 g	butter
4		eggs
1 Tbsp	15 mL	vanilla extract
¼ tsp	1 mL	baking soda
¼ cup	35 g	instant flour (see Brownie Point on page 44)
½ tsp	2 mL	kosher salt
1 cup	120 g	walnuts, finely chopped
1 cup	250 mL	unsweetened whipped cream or crème fraîche

1. Preheat the oven to 300°F (150°C). Line a 9- x 9-inch (23- x 23-cm) baking pan with overhanging parchment paper.

2. Place the dates, water and honey in a medium saucepan over medium heat.

3. Bring to a boil, then turn down to a simmer.

4. Stir and mash the cooked dates with a rubber spatula until you have a smooth purée. Remove from the heat.

5. Add the chocolate and butter and mix until both are melted.

6. Add the eggs one a time and mix until well blended. Add the vanilla.

7. Stir in the baking soda.

8. Add the flour and salt and mix. The batter will be thick.

9. Spread into the prepared pan.

10. Sprinkle the finely chopped nuts evenly over the surface and gently press to make them adhere.

11. Bake for 30 minutes. The center will puff up. Don't overbake!

12. Let cool. Slice and serve with unsweetened whipped cream or crème fraîche.

INNER peace caramel brownies

YIELD: 16 BARS

These are pure flavor. The deep, thick chocolate batter is glossy going into the oven and stays that way until it's time to come out. These are major fudgy, to the point of being wet at the center. Cool in the fridge for an even fudgier texture. The darker the caramel, the edgier (slightly more bitter) the flavor. The first time around, don't go too dark, then be daring! They taste superb served warm with a scoop of vanilla ice cream.

caramel:

1 ¾ cups	175 g	**sugar**
¼ cup	60 mL	**water**
8 Tbsp	115 g	**butter**
¾ cup	175 g	**sugar**
4 oz	112 g	**bittersweet chocolate, chopped**
1 recipe		**Caramel, cooled**
3		**eggs**
1 tsp	5 mL	**vanilla extract**
¼ tsp	1 mL	**kosher salt**
¾ cups	100 g	**all-purpose flour**

1. Set aside a bowl of ice water big enough to hold a 6-inch (15-cm) saucepan.

2. Place the sugar and water in the saucepan over medium heat.

3. Bring to a boil, stirring to dissolve the sugar. Use a pastry brush dipped in cold water to brush down any sugar crystals on the side of the pan, or cover the pan briefly so the steam created inside the pot can dissolve any crystals.

4. Boil the sugar until it starts to caramelize. Watch it carefully, because a few things happen. In some pans, caramelization will occur on one side of the pan before the other; in this instance, swirl the pot gently to get an even color. In other pans, once the sugar begins to brown, it goes from light to dark very quickly and will continue to cook even when removed from the heat. When the sugar has become a medium chestnut brown (it should really be brown, but not dark), remove from the heat and immediately set the bottom of the pan into the bowl of ice water. This will stop the cooking. If you don't think it's quite brown enough, remove it from the heat, watch it carefully and when it gets to the desired color, set it in the ice water.

5. Preheat the oven to 350°F (180°C) Line an 8- x 8-inch (20- x 20-cm) pan with overhanging parchment paper.

6. In a medium saucepan, melt the butter with the sugar. Remove from the heat and add the chocolate. Stir until it is melted and the mixture is thick and glossy.

7. Add the cooled caramel and mix thoroughly.

8. Break the eggs into a small bowl and whisk lightly. Add all at once to the chocolate mixture and whisk until smooth and glossy.

9. Add the vanilla and salt. Mix to blend.

10. Add the flour and mix only enough to blend.

11. Pour into the prepared pan and bake for 25–30 minutes.

12. Remove and cool completely.

peanut butter brownie bars

YIELD: 16 BARS

No matter how I try to stay away from the chocolate-nut combination, and the chocolate-peanut combination in particular, my mind keeps creating new ways to wed these two well-suited mates. The earthiness of peanuts contrasts with chocolate so that the flavors neither stand apart nor merge into one. It's truly a marriage made in heaven.

BROWNIE BOTTOM:

1 oz	28 g	**unsweetened chocolate**
5 oz	140 g	**bittersweet chocolate**
¼ cup + 2 Tbsp	90 mL	**peanut butter at room temperature**
4 Tbsp	55 g	**butter at room temperature**
½ cup	110 g	**brown sugar**
2		**eggs**
¼ cup	35 g	**whole wheat flour**
½ tsp	2 mL	**kosher salt**
6 oz	170 g	**bittersweet chocolate, chopped**
1 recipe		**Peanut Butter Topping**
1 cup	250 mL	**Ganache (page 28), liquid but cool**

1. Preheat the oven to 300°F (150°C). Line a 8- x 8-inch (20- x 20-cm) pan with overhanging parchment paper.

2. Place the chocolates in a microwavable bowl. Microwave for 1 minute, check, stir and microwave again for about 1 more minute, being careful to not burn the chocolate.

3. In the bowl of an electric mixer, beat the peanut butter and butter until soft.

4. Add the sugar and beat until blended.

5. Add both melted chocolates, mixing for about 1 minute and scraping the bottom and sides of the bowl from time to time.

6. Add the eggs, mixing to blend.

7. Whisk together the flour and salt.

8. Add to the bowl and mix on low speed for about 1 minute.

9. Fold in the chopped chocolate. The batter will be thick.

10. Spread into the prepared pan and bake for about 30 minutes. The brownie will feel soft to the touch but will firm up as it cools. Cool completely.

11. Spread Peanut Butter Topping over the cooled brownies. Place in the refrigerator to set.

12. Pour the ganache over the brownie slab. Tilt the rack in a circular motion to spread the ganache. Let set.

13. Place the brownie slab on a cutting board. Cut with a thin knife, heating it under hot water and drying it between each slice.

14. Store tightly covered in the fridge for up to 3 weeks.

peanut butter topping:

¾ cup	190 mL	**peanut butter**
8 Tbsp	115 g	**butter**
½ cup	60 g	**icing sugar**
½ tsp	2 mL	**ground cardamom**
¼ tsp	1 mL	**kosher salt**

1. Place all the ingredients in the bowl of a food processor. Process until smooth.

NO Bake BROWNies

YIELD: 24 BARS

I don't know whether these are brownies or candy, but whichever they are, they're hard to beat in both taste and ease of preparation. The next time you need something to impress the boss or win kudos at the bake sale, bring these!

7 oz	200 g	**bittersweet chocolate, chopped**
1 pound	454 g	**milk chocolate, chopped**
4 Tbsp	55 g	**butter**
10		**marshmallows**
¾ cup	175 mL	**corn syrup**
2 cups	500 mL	**peanut butter**
½ cup	110 g	**brown sugar**
4 oz	112 g	**peanuts, chopped**
3 cups	100 g	**crispy rice cereal**
1 cup	250 mL	**Ganache (optional, page 28)**

1. Line a 9- x 13-inch (23- x 33-cm) pan with overhanging parchment paper.

2. In a large, heavy saucepan over medium-low heat, melt both chocolates and the butter.

3. Add the marshmallows. Stir until the marshmallows and chocolate are completely melted.

4. Remove from the heat and stir in the corn syrup, peanut butter and brown sugar. Mix until smooth, about 1 minute.

5. Add the peanuts and rice cereal, mixing lightly but thoroughly.

6. Pour into the prepared pan and smooth with a spatula.

7. Let set or place in the fridge to firm up.

8. If you are glazing the bars, warm the Ganache until pourable, about 80–85°F (27–30°C). Pour it in a steady stream over the center of the brownie slab in the pan. It will spread out towards the sides in a circular pattern.

9. Lift the pan and tilt from side to side until the entire surface is covered with a smooth and glossy glaze. Cool completely.

10. To remove from the pan, wet a sponge under hot water and press it against the sides of the brownie pan. You will see the glaze melt around the edges as you move the sponge along the sides.

11. Gently lift the slab by the overhanging parchment and place it on a cutting board to slice.

12. Store in the fridge, well wrapped, for 3 weeks or in the freezer for 3 months.

BROWNie POINt

Here's an even faster version. Melt both chocolates. While they're melting, in a large bowl, combine the peanuts (or any other nut, for that matter), 1 cup (120 g) raisins (or any other dried fruit cut to the same size as a raisin), crispy rice cereal (or substitute a bran cereal for something a tad healthier), and the marshmallows cut into pieces the size of raisins. Pour in the melted chocolate and mix gently with a rubber spatula, coating everything with the chocolate. To complete you have two options: either drop by tablespoons onto a parchment-lined baking sheet and let cool completely or press into a 9- x 13-inch (23- x 33-cm) parchment-lined pan and cut into bars before the chocolate has solidified completely. Store in a tightly sealed container for about a week.

oozy walnut bars

YIELD: 24 BARS

I love pecan pie but it needs chocolate. In this recipe, I've added chocolate in the form of Mascarpone Chocolate Curd—just in case there wasn't enough richness for you—and used walnuts instead of pecans for their slight bitterness. Good walnuts are hard to find. Bad ones, alas, are not only easy to pick up everywhere, but they also destroy anything you put them in, so taste before you buy. Don't be frugal. Buy good California walnuts or risk spoiling this fabulous bittersweet filling. The baking method is, to say the least, unorthodox and resulted when I started the recipe only to realize I had to be at work in 10 minutes. So I turned the oven off after 10 minutes baking and returned at the end of the day to perfectly oozy bars. If you want to bake them to the end, bake for no longer than 20 minutes; otherwise, just let the warmth of the oven do its job while you go out to do yours!

1 cup	300 g	**Pâte Sucrée au Chocolat (page 22)**
1 cup	250 mL	**Mascarpone Chocolate Curd (page 26)**
½ cup	110 g	brown sugar
½ cup	125 mL	corn syrup
2		eggs
½ tsp	2 mL	salt
12 oz	300 g	whole walnuts or large pieces

1. Preheat the oven to 350°F (180°C). Line a 9- x 13-inch (23- x 33-cm) pan with overhanging parchment paper.

2. Press the Pâte Sucrée au Chocolat into the prepared pan in an even but thin layer. Refrigerate 10 minutes.

3. Bake for 10 minutes.

4. While the crust is baking, whisk together the curd, sugar, corn syrup, eggs and salt.

5. Remove the crust from the oven. Pour the filling over the crust and sprinkle with the nuts.

6. Place in the oven and set the timer for 10 minutes.

7. After 10 minutes, turn the oven off and let the residual heat of the oven finish the baking. After an hour, you can remove the pan.

8. Let cool completely before cutting into squares.

BROWNIE POINT

These bars, with their thin crust, are fragile when still warm and may crumble when sliced. For easier slicing, chill completely, then let come to room temperature before serving.

For Boozy Walnut Bars, add 2 Tbsp (30 mL) bourbon whisky to the eggs before mixing with the Mascarpone Curd.

peanut butter crunch brownies

YIELD: 16 BARS AND 12 COOKIES

This recipe occurred to me after making a fresh peach crumble with a cornmeal and almond topping. I thought about making a peanut butter crumble and then decided to make my favorite peanut butter cookie recipe combined with a brownie recipe. The result is at once fudgy and smooth, crunchy on the top and inside. Best at room temperature and enjoyed with your choice of milk or coffee. You'll have some peanut butter cookie batter left over to turn into cookies or roll and freeze for future baking.

8 Tbsp	112 g	**butter at room temperature**
1 cup	250 mL	**smooth or chunky peanut butter**
½ cup	100 g	**granulated sugar**
¾ cup	165 g	**brown sugar**
2		**eggs**
2 cups	260 g	**all-purpose flour**
½ tsp	2 mL	**baking soda**
½ tsp	2 mL	**baking powder**
¼ tsp	1 mL	**kosher salt**
4 oz	112 g	**dry-roasted peanuts, coarsely chopped**
3 cups	750 mL	**Classic Brownie (page 42), First and Foremost Brownie (page 41), or Cruise Ship Brownie (page 52) batter**
		icing sugar for dusting

1. Preheat the oven to 350°F (180°C). Line a baking sheet with parchment paper. Line an 8- x 8-inch (20- x 20-cm) pan with overhanging parchment paper.

2. Combine the butter and peanut butter in the bowl of an electric mixer. Set over a pan of simmering water and stir until the butter has melted and the two ingredients are combined.

3. Remove from the heat and place the bowl on the mixer. Add both sugars and mix until smooth.

4. Add the eggs, beating them in one at a time and scraping the bowl between additions.

5. Combine the flour, baking soda, baking powder and salt. Add to the peanut butter mixture and mix until just combined.

6. Add the nuts and mix.

7. Divide the dough roughly into thirds. You will use one-third for Cookie Bites and one-third for crumble. Use the last portion to make 12 cookies. (Place the dough on a sheet of parchment paper. Roll the paper around the dough and roll gently to form a cylinder about 12 inches [30 cm] long. Twist both ends of the paper closed and wrap the roll in plastic wrap. Store in the fridge or freezer. When ready to bake, cut in ½-inch [1.25-cm] slices and place on a parchment-lined baking sheet. Use a fork to press a crisscross pattern lightly on top. Bake at 350°F [180°C] for about 12 minutes.)

8. To make the Cookie Bites, pinch off walnut-sized blobs of dough and place on the parchment-lined baking sheet. You will have about 16 pieces.

9. Bake for about 10–12 minutes or until they show some color. They will not be crisp until they have cooled.

10. When the Cookie Bites are completely cool, carefully fold them into the brownie batter, taking care not to overmix and break them up. You want them to stay in their original shape.

11. Pour the batter into the prepared pan and gently smooth the top.

12. Crumble the remaining ⅓ of the dough evenly between your fingers over the brownie batter to create a nice crunchy topping.

13. Bake for 25–30 minutes. The batter shouldn't jiggle, but it shouldn't be puffed up, either. The crumble will be golden brown on top and firm.

14. Remove from the oven and cool completely in the pan. Lift out of the pan holding both sides of the parchment paper.

15. When completely cool, dust the top with icing sugar.

16. Cut into slices with a wet knife, wiping it clean after every slice.

17. Store tightly covered in the fridge for up to a week. The crumble will get less crunchy over time.

BROWNIE POINT

Instead of dusting with icing sugar, drizzle Ganache (page 28) on top or drizzle with lemon glaze: ¼ cup (60 mL) icing sugar mixed until smooth with 2–3 tsp (10-15 mL) lemon juice.

pecan shortbread caramel brownies

YIELD: 24 BARS

As a kid, I used to go to Schrafft's in New York City with my Grandma Mae, for lunch. I'd be thrown into a state of paralyzing indecision when it came to dessert: should I have the hot fudge sundae with gooey, warm fudge cascading down a mountain of vanilla ice cream, or should I glory in the butterscotch sundae, warm butterscotch sailing down a smooth slope of vanilla ice cream, but with "skis" of salted nuts on the slopes? I remember having both, though not at the same time, of course. So in this brownie, I combine the two memories into one sensational bar: fudgy chocolate and gooey caramel.

shortbread Layer:

1 cup	227 g	butter
¾ cup + 1 Tbsp	180 g	brown sugar
½ tsp	2 mL	kosher salt
3 cups	360 g	pastry flour
2 Tbsp	30 mL	rice flour

BROWNIE POINT

You can substitute any brownie batter for the marshmallow brownie batter. You can use Pâte Sucrée au Chocolat (page 22) in place of the shortbread crust, if you have any on hand, for a double hit of chocolate. If you don't have any caramel sauce, make a quick substitute by mixing together ½ tin (160 mL) of sweetened condensed milk with 2 Tbsp (30 mL) melted butter and 2 Tbsp (30 mL) brown sugar. Add 4 oz (112 g) pecans and stir to coat. Gently spread over the brownies during the last 10 minutes of baking. Bake until bubbly and slightly golden.

1. Preheat the oven to 300°F (150°C). Line a 9- x 9-inch (23- x 23-cm) baking pan with overhanging parchment paper.

2. In the bowl of an electric mixer fitted with the paddle attachment, beat the butter until smooth.

3. Add the sugar and salt. Beat on low speed until well combined, scraping the sides and bottom of the bowl from time to time.

4. Add both flours and beat on low. The mix will look pebbly and won't initially come together. Have no fear!

5. Scrape the sides and bottom of the bowl after 1 minute, turn the mixer on low and mix until the dough just comes together.

6. Remove half the dough and roll it into a cylinder about 1 inch (2.5 cm) in diameter. Wrap in plastic and store in the fridge. This is your extra half. To make shortbread cookies, slice in ¼-inch (5-mm) rounds and bake for about 10 minutes at 300°F (150°C) until barely browned.

7. Pat the remaining dough into the prepared pan. Bake for 20 minutes until light brown.

marshmallow brownie Layer:

8 Tbsp	115 g	**butter**
¼ cup	30 g	**cocoa**
¾ cup	150 g	**granulated sugar**
4		**large marshmallows**
2		**eggs**
½ tsp	2 mL	**vanilla extract**
		pinch salt
⅓ cup	45 g	**all-purpose flour**
4 oz	112 g	**toasted pecans**
2 Tbsp	30 mL	**Caramel Butterscotch Sauce, homemade (page 32) or storebought**
		sprinkle kosher salt

1. Melt the butter over low heat in a medium saucepan.

2. Add the cocoa and stir to moisten.

3. Add the sugar and stir until it melts and becomes liquid, although it will still be grainy.

4. Add the marshmallows and stir until completely melted.

5. Remove the pan from the heat and let cool for 5 minutes.

6. Add the eggs one at a time, beating until the batter is thick and glossy.

7. Add the vanilla and salt.

8. Add the flour and mix just enough to blend thoroughly.

9. Spread the batter over the baked shortbread crust.

10. Return to the oven and bake for 20 minutes.

11. Remove from the oven and spread the pecans evenly over the top.

12. Drizzle with Caramel Butterscotch Sauce and sprinkle with the salt.

13. Return to the oven for an additional 10 minutes or until the sauce starts to bubble.

14. Cool completely before lifting out of the pan to slice.

triple espresso brownies

YIELD: 24 BARS

I grew up in the coffee business and started drinking coffee at age 12 when I read an article in the *New York Times* that said coffee consumption was down. I thought my entry into the market would be good for my dad's business. Little did I know that years later I'd be running Canada's second-largest coffee company! Coffee and chocolate are one of those food combinations that go together because they grow together. They share a similar but not identical terroir, or geography. This brownie adds a twist of lemon to the filling, just like an Italian espresso. Don't substitute instant coffee for the real thing here. Start the ganache, then make the cream cheese filling and finally the batter. This makes enough for a crowd.

espresso ganache:

10 oz	280 g	**bittersweet chocolate, chopped**
7 oz	196 g	**white chocolate, chopped**
1 cup	250 mL	**whipping cream**
1 Tbsp	15 mL	**freshly ground espresso powder**
		pinch kosher salt

1. Place both chocolates in a bowl.
2. Place the cream and espresso powder in a small saucepan set over medium heat. Bring to just below the boil, when bubbles appear around the edges of the surface.
3. Remove from the heat and let steep while you make the cream cheese filling and the brownies.
4. When the brownies are in the oven, finish the ganache by reheating the cream to just below the boil.
5. Pour over the chopped chocolates and let sit for 5 minutes. Whisk until smooth. Whisk in the salt.
6. Set aside until the brownies are ready for glazing.

lemon cream cheese filling:

8 oz	227 g	**cream cheese**
1		**lemon, zest grated**
2 Tbsp	30 mL	**lemon juice**
¼ cup	50 g	**sugar**
2		**eggs**

1. Place all the ingredients in the bowl of a food processor and whip until smooth. Pour into a bowl and set aside while you prepare the brownies.

tRiple espResso BROWNie Batter:

9 oz	250 g	**bittersweet chocolate, chopped**
2 oz	56 g	**unsweetened chocolate, chopped**
12 Tbsp	170 g	**butter**
2 cups	400 g	**sugar**
4 Tbsp	60 mL	**freshly ground espresso powder, divided**
4		**eggs**
½ cup	65 g	**all-purpose flour**
		pinch kosher salt

1. Preheat the oven to 300°F (150°C). Line a 9- x 13-inch (23- x 33-cm) baking pan with overhanging parchment paper.

2. Place both chocolates in a medium-sized bowl over a pot of simmering water.

3. Add the butter and whisk from time to time until smooth and completely melted.

4. Add the sugar and 2 Tbsp. (30 mL) of the espresso powder. Whisk to blend. It will be granular in appearance.

5. Remove from the heat. Cool 10 minutes.

6. Whisk in the eggs one at a time. Because the batter is still warm, it is important to whisk quickly. Adding the eggs will thicken the batter.

7. Whisk in the flour and salt, mixing only enough to blend well.

8. Pour half the batter into the prepared pan. Drizzle half the Lemon Cream Cheese filling over the brownie base. Spoon the remaining brownie batter over the cream cheese and spread gently to the corners, covering the cream cheese. Drizzle the remaining cream cheese batter over the brownie. It may sink. Don't worry.

9. Bake for 30 minutes. The brownie will appear puffed and jiggly.

10. Remove from the oven. Let it cool for about an hour.

11. Pour the ganache on top and sprinkle with the remaining 2 Tbsp (30 mL) espresso powder.

12. Place in the fridge to cool completely.

13. Use the parchment paper to lift out the brownie slab and slice.

rye almond brownies

YIELD: 16 BARS

In my attempt to appeal to people on one diet or another, I've tried all sorts of recipes with varying degrees of success. When you take things out of brownies, like the fat or the sugar, and replace them with something else, they may look like a brownie, but they sure don't taste like it! This recipe reduces the gluten and is for people seeking to replace wheat in their diet. It looks and tastes just like a "regular" brownie, but with something elusive about it.

10 Tbsp	140 g	**butter**
1 cup	120 g	**cocoa**
1 ¼ cups	250 g	**sugar**
¼ tsp	1 mL	**kosher salt**
1 tsp	5 mL	**instant coffee granules**
½ tsp	2 mL	**vanilla extract**
¼ tsp	1 mL	**almond extract**
2		**eggs**
½ cup	60 g	**rye flour**
1 oz	28 g	**almonds, toasted and ground**

1. Preheat the oven to 300°F (150°C). Line a 9- x 9-inch (23- x 23-cm) baking pan with overhanging parchment paper.

2. Melt the butter in a medium saucepan. Add the cocoa and whisk until smooth. Let sit for 5 minutes.

3. Whisk in the sugar, salt, coffee and extracts.

4. Add the eggs and whisk until smooth.

5. Mix the flour with the almonds and whisk into the chocolate mixture.

6. Pour into the prepared pan and bake for 25 minutes.

7. Cool and slice.

brownie point

Kamut flour is a grain that is lower in gluten than wheat, although not entirely gluten free. Still, it has great flavor and can replace the rye in this recipe. You can also substitute 1 cup (220 g) brown sugar for the white.

bitter bitter chocolate brownies

(aka JIMBO'S 80TH BIRTHDAY "cake")

YIELD: 16 BARS

My dad and I used to see the New York Giants when they played at Yankee Stadium. I loved being with him, and I loved the great hot dogs we'd get at a deli underneath the "El" (elevated subway) and the chocolate bars that would crack when we ate them because it was so cold outside. To this day, my dad loves chocolate, so there was nothing more fitting than this dessert for his 80th birthday, celebrated among family and friends. There's a high percentage of bitter chocolate relative to the amount of sugar—I wanted to make an "adult" brownie with a deep chocolate flavor.

At first the taste is surprisingly bitter, but as it warms in your mouth (or if you eat it warm) the true essence of chocolate comes to the fore. These are superb with vanilla ice cream.

6 ½ oz	180 g	unsweetened chocolate
8 Tbsp	115 g	butter
¾ cup	150 g	granulated sugar
3		eggs
1 Tbsp	15 mL	vanilla extract
1 Tbsp	15 mL	instant coffee granules
¼ tsp	1 mL	kosher salt
½ cup	65 g	all-purpose flour

1. Preheat the oven to 300°F (150°C). Line an 8- x 8-inch (20- x 20-cm) pan with parchment paper

2. In a medium saucepan, melt the chocolate and butter.

3. Add the sugar and stir over very low heat until it is almost all dissolved, about 10 minutes.

4. Remove from the heat and cool for about 10 minutes before adding the eggs.

5. Whisk the eggs with the vanilla and gradually add to the chocolate mixture, stirring constantly so they don't cook.

6. Add the instant coffee and salt and mix well.

7. Stir in the flour, blending until just incorporated.

8. Pour into the prepared pan and bake for 30 minutes.

9. Remove from the oven and serve warm with vanilla ice cream and nothing else!

caramel Ganache Bittersweet brownies

YIELD: 16 BARS

1 recipe		**baked, chilled Bitter Bitter Chocolate Brownies (previous page), in the pan**
½ cup	125 mL	**Caramel Butterscotch Sauce (page 32)**
½ cup	125 mL	**Ganache (page 28)**
16		**toasted pecans (optional)**
		sea salt (optional)

1. Spread the Caramel Butterscotch Sauce over the top of the chilled brownie.

2. Place in the freezer for 30 minutes.

3. Warm the Ganache to the point where it is just pourable and barely warm to the touch, about 80–85°F (27–30°C).

4. Remove the brownies from the freezer and pour the Ganache in a pool in the center of the pan. Quickly spread the chocolate to the edges in as few strokes as possible.

5. Top with the toasted pecans placed in 4 x 4 rows so each bar gets a pecan.

6. Sprinkle very lightly with fine sea salt, if desired.

7. Slice and serve!

BROWNIE POINT

Many brownie recipes call for melting butter and unsweetened chocolate together as a first step and then adding sugar and eggs. If the mixture is too hot, the fat may separate from the chocolate, leaving a shiny film on top. In this case, like making mayonnaise, you need to reincorporate the fat (also known as emulsifying) back into the other ingredients. This is best achieved through rapid whisking and/or cooling. Or, try whisking in a small amount (1 Tbsp/15 mL) of chopped chocolate to bring down the temperature. Don't add your eggs unless the chocolate and butter look thick and glossy and fully incorporated.

raspberry brownies

YIELD: 16 BROWNIES

Yum! That is almost all I can say about these brownies. Dense, fudgy and intense with real raspberry flavor.

1 pint	150 g	fresh raspberries
1 Tbsp	15 mL	granulated sugar
8 oz	227 g	unsweetened chocolate
1 cup	227 g	butter
2 cups	400 g	granulated sugar
½ cup	110 g	brown sugar
4		eggs
⅛ tsp	0.5 mL	salt
½ cup	65 g	all-purpose flour
1 ½ cups	325 mL	Ganache (page 28)

1. To make the raspberry purée, place the raspberries and the 1 Tbsp (15 g) sugar in a small saucepan. Add 1 Tbsp (15 mL) of water and place over low heat. Mash the raspberries with a wooden spoon or rubber spatula.

2. Bring to a boil, then lower the heat. Cook until you have a thickened sauce. Be careful it doesn't burn!

3. Place mixture in a sieve and press it through with a spatula. You should have about 1 cup (250 mL) of seedless purée.

4. Preheat the oven to 300°F (150°C). Line a 9- x 9-inch (23- x 23-cm) pan with parchment paper.

5. Melt the chocolate and butter over low heat. Blend well.

6. Add the 2 cups (400 g) granulated sugar and the brown sugar. Mix until both are almost completely dissolved.

7. Add the eggs one at a time, beating until completely smooth and glossy.

8. Add the salt and *half* the raspberry purée. Blend well.

9. Add the flour and mix just enough to blend.

10. Pour into the prepared pan and bake for 30 minutes.

11. Remove from the oven and cool completely.

12. If necessary, warm the Ganache in the microwave on medium power or over barely boiling water until just melted, about 80–85°F (27–30°C).

13. Add the remaining raspberry purée to the Ganache and whisk until smooth.

14. Pour mixture over the brownies and tilt the pan to spread the Ganache smoothly.

15. Let sit until the glaze is set. Cut and serve!

brownie points

Top each brownie with a fresh raspberry.

soft AND aromatic
Brownie Cakes

3

CRANBERRY GANACHE CRUMBLE FLAN p. 146

A Quartet of Brownies: from top clockwise: JACKSON POLLOCK BARS p. 60, NO BAKE BROWNIES p. 66, CHOCOLATE RASPBERRY PEANUT BUTTER CRUMBLE BARS p. 48, FIVE NUTS IN A PAN BROWNIES p. 54

Lemon marble stack cake p. 92

chocolate espresso coffee cake p. 98

BROWNIE PECAN TORTE

YIELD: 10–12 SERVINGS

This was a desperation recipe. I arrived home after being away for five days, rising at 4 a.m. every day to work in a bakery. Needless to say, all I wanted to do was sleep, but I was expected at someone's house for dinner and had to provide dessert. Checking the freezer, I identified a patient slab of foil-wrapped brownies I had made easily a month earlier. I grabbed some clearly marked Mocha Ganache, toasted some pecans, and had a beautiful and elegant torte in less than 20 minutes. You can, too, if you keep your freezer stocked with the components.

1 recipe		Cocoa Brownies (page 50), baked in a 9- x 9-inch (23- x 23-cm) pan
2 cups	500 mL	Mocha Ganache (page 99)
2 cups	250 g	toasted pecans, ground medium fine in a food processor and placed on a cookie sheet

BROWNIE POINT

The parchment-lined cookie sheet with a rack set over it enables you to pour a glorious layer of glaze over the torte without worrying that you are wasting a huge amount. It allows you to create a smooth surface. Whatever is left in the pan can be heated gently, strained of any errant crumbs and saved for another use.

1. Cut the brownie slab in half so you have two slabs 4 ½ inches (11 cm) wide.

2. Line a cookie sheet with parchment paper. Place a rack over the parchment. Cut a piece of cardboard 4 ½ x 9 inches (11 x 23 cm) and place on the rack to support the cake.

3. Place one of the brownie slabs, bottom side up, on the cardboard.

4. Warm the ganache in the microwave to about 80–85°F (27–30°C) so it has the consistency of thick paint—creamy but slightly resistant when stirred.

5. Pour a generous amount over the center of the bottom slab. When it spreads to the edges, stop pouring and use a metal spatula or tilt the entire rack, holding onto the slab with your thumbs, to gently coax the ganache to cover the sides. Chill in the fridge for 15 minutes until firm. You want the ganache to harden into a layer that will support the next slab, so don't be in too much of a hurry or make the ganache too warm.

6. Place the second slab over the first, aligning the edges.

7. Pour the remaining ganache over the center of the torte and spread lightly so that it falls down the sides. You should have enough glaze to cover the entire top. Gently smooth the sides to fill in any space between the two slabs. If glaze continues to dribble down the sides, keep smoothing it into any crevices.

8. Using a long spatula, lift the torte off the rack and place it in the palm of one hand. Hold over the cookie sheet with the pecans. Using your free hand, scoop up a handful of nuts and gently press them into and up the sides of the torte, leaving a slight edge of pecans over the top rim.

9. Turn the torte in your hand or put it down and turn it before lifting it again in order to pat the nuts into all four sides. Let the excess nuts fall back into the pan. Voila! Brownie Pecan Torte!

the ultimate brownie cheesecake

or cheesecake brownie

YIELD: 8 SERVINGS

I couldn't decide if I wanted a brownie with a lot of cheesecake or a cheesecake with a lot of brownie. In fact, out of these two recipes comes the possibility of three different desserts: one, a true cheesecake with a "crust" of brownie; a brownie with a wonderful layer of cheesecake; or a combination of the two, truly marbled and, to my mind, the best of all. But you be the judge. Having the brownie batter on hand will save you time. You'll have more cheesecake batter than you need for any of these recipes individually. You can make a larger 10-inch (25-cm) Brownie Cheesecake by increasing the brownie batter base to 3 cups (750 mL). You can also use the leftover cheesecake batter to make mini-cheesecakes in cupcake tins. Or, increase the brownie batter to 4 cups (1 L) and make two 8-inch (20-cm) Brownie Cheesecakes instead of one. Keep one in the freezer for emergencies. Well wrapped in plastic and foil, it will last for months.

2 cups	500 mL	Classic Brownie batter (page 42)
8 oz	227 g	cream cheese
2		eggs
¼ cup	50 g	sugar
2 Tbsp	30 mL	heavy cream
1 Tbsp	15 mL	lemon juice
1		lemon, grated zest
2 tsp	10 mL	vanilla extract
⅛ tsp	0.5 mL	salt
for dusting		icing sugar, cocoa
for garnish		berries

1. Preheat oven to 300°F (150°C). Wrap foil tightly around the bottom of an 8-inch (20-cm) springform pan. Spray the pan with vegetable spray and line the bottom with a round of parchment paper.

2. Spread the Classic Brownie batter evenly onto the bottom of the pan.

3. Place all the remaining ingredients in the bowl of a food processor fitted with the steel blade.

4. Process until smooth, scraping the bottom and sides to dislodge any unwhipped pieces of cream cheese.

5. Pour 2-3 cups (500-750 mL) of batter over the brownie base in the pan. The amount you use is determined by the answer to this question: Do you want substantially more cheesecake than brownie or not? Whichever way you decide, spread it smoothly.

6. Bake for approximately 30-40 minutes, then raise the temperature to 350°F (180°C) for an additional 15-20 minutes, until the cake is slightly puffed but not at all browned on top. The center should be slightly jiggly but not fluid underneath the surface. Tap it lightly with your finger to see if it is done.

7. Turn off the oven, open the oven door and cool for about 20 minutes.

8. Remove from the oven and cool completely before placing it in the fridge overnight.

9. To unmold the chilled cake, run a paring knife around the edge of the pan. Place the pan over low heat and move around in circles so that the heat is applied evenly to the bottom of the pan. This should take no more than 10 seconds. Run the tip of a knife around the edges of the cake to loosen. Remove the side of the springform pan and slide a wide spatula underneath the parchment paper. The cake will slide easily off the pan and onto a serving plate.

10. Dust lightly with cocoa and icing sugar and garnish with berries.

brownie point

For extra richness and pizzazz, completely chill the cake in the pan. Pour ½ cup (125 mL) slightly warmed ganache over the top. Tip the cake to and fro to spread the ganache just to the edges. To remove from the pan, first warm the bottom over low heat on the stove for about 10 seconds, no more. Warm a paring knife under hot water and wipe dry. Run the tip of the paring knife around the edge of the cake to loosen from the pan. Remove the springform and slide the cake onto a serving dish. Cut with a piece of dental floss or a long, thin knife run under hot water and wiped dry.

steamed brownie cheesecake puddings

If you are short of time, try these. You get the same brownie cheesecake hit in a fraction of the time. Spray four espresso cups or 4-oz (125-mL) ramekins with vegetable spray. Set them in an 8- x 8-inch (20- x 20-cm) pan. Preheat the oven to 300°F (150°C). Bring a pot of water to a boil. Fill each ramekin half full with brownie batter. Fill to just below the top with cheesecake batter. Place the brownie pan with the cups on the shelf in the oven. Carefully pour the boiling water halfway up the sides of the cups. Cover the pan tightly with foil but tent it to leave room for the custards to puff without sticking to the foil. Steam in the oven for about 15 minutes, or until the tops are slightly puffed. Remove from the oven and serve warm. These little puddings are incredibly rich and smooth without being too heavy.

cheesecake brownies

YIELD: 24 BARS

Prepare the brownie and cheesecake batter as for Brownie Cheesecake (page 82).

1. Preheat oven to 300°F (150°C). Line an 8- x 8-inch (20- x 20-cm) pan with overhanging parchment paper.

2. Spread 2 cups (500 mL) of brownie batter evenly in the pan.

3. Pour 1 recipe of cheesecake batter over the brownie batter and spread to cover the brownies.

4. Bake for about 30-40 minutes, or until the cheesecake is firm but still moist.

5. Remove from the oven, cool and chill completely overnight.

6. Run a knife around the edges of the pan to loosen. Carefully warm the bottom of the baking pan on the stove for about 15 seconds. Gently lift the two sides of parchment up and out of the pan, being careful to keep the slab as flat as possible. This is a very custardy brownie, so it will be fragile. Place on a cutting board and cut with a wet knife wiped clean after every slice.

7. Store wrapped in foil in the fridge for up to three weeks.

marble brownies

YIELD: 24 BARS

Prepare the brownie and cheesecake batters as for Brownie Cheesecake (page 82).

1. Preheat the oven to 300°F (150°C). Line an 8- x 8-inch (20- x 20-cm) pan with overhanging parchment paper.

2. Pour the cheesecake batter into the pan, spreading it level.

3. Pour 2 cups (500 mL) of brownie batter in a random pattern over the cheesecake batter. It will sink in at first, but as you continue and overlap, it will begin to surface.

4. Place in the oven for 30–40 minutes, or until just firm.

5. Remove from the oven, cool and chill completely.

6. Lift out of the pan and cut into the desired size by dipping a knife in hot water and wiping after every slice.

7. These will last a good month stored in foil in the fridge.

chocolate ginger brownie cake

YIELD: 12 SERVINGS

My dad loves gingerbread, and since he and my mom dine with us every Sunday night, I'm always on the lookout for great gingerbread recipes. One day I found one, in *Room for Dessert* by David Lebovitz. It's moist and succulent but, based on my theory that everything can be improved by the addition of chocolate, I went to work. I hope David will forgive me for tinkering with his recipe. The result is gingery and brownie-like in flavor if not exactly fudgy in texture. Glazed with a Ginger-Infused Ganache, it's wonderful with vanilla ice cream or unsweetened whipped cream.

¾ cup	110 g	all-purpose flour
¼ cup	30 g	cocoa
½ tsp	2 mL	baking soda
¼ tsp	1 mL	salt
2 Tbsp	30 mL	butter
1 oz	28 g	bittersweet chocolate
¼ cup + 2 tsp	60 g	granulated sugar
¼ cup	55 g	brown sugar
3 Tbsp	45 mL	vegetable oil
¼ cup	60 mL	molasses
1		egg
2–3 Tbsp	28 g	peeled, chopped fresh ginger
2–3 Tbsp	28 g	finely diced candied ginger
2 oz	56 g	bittersweet chocolate, finely chopped
½ cup	125 mL	hot water or coffee
1 cup	250 mL	Ginger-Infused Ganache (optional)

1. Preheat the oven to 350°F. (180°C). Grease the bottom and sides of an 8-inch (20-cm) round or square pan.

2. Mix the flour, cocoa, baking soda and salt and set aside.

3. In a small saucepan, melt the butter and the 1 oz (28 g) chocolate. Stir to blend.

4. In a medium bowl, whisk together both sugars, oil, molasses and egg. Whisk until smooth.

5. Add the melted butter and chocolate, mixing until smooth.

6. Add both gingers and the finely chopped chocolate.

7. Add the dry ingredients, mixing only until the flour disappears and the batter is smooth.

8. Add the hot water or coffee and mix it in completely. The batter will be fairly thin.

9. Pour into the prepared pan and bake for about 40–50 minutes or until firm and springy to the touch.

10. Let the cake cool completely before glazing with the ganache.

11. To glaze, place the cake on a rack set over a cookie pan lined with parchment paper. Pour the ganache from about 1 inch (2.5 cm) above the center of the cake. It should pool and spread evenly over the top and sides. Don't use a spatula to spread the top if you can avoid it, but do use it to mask the sides with glaze. Let the glaze cool completely before serving.

12. The unglazed cake may be wrapped in plastic and stored in the fridge for about 2 weeks. Wrapped with plastic, then foil, store in the freezer for up to 6 months.

ginger-infused ganache:

YIELD: 2¼ CUPS (560 mL)

8 oz	227 g	**bittersweet chocolate, chopped**
2 ½ Tbsp	37 mL	**fresh ginger, peeled and finely chopped**
1 cup	250 mL	**whipping cream**
1 Tbsp	15 mL	**corn syrup**
1 Tbsp	15 mL	**butter**

1. Place the chocolate in a mixing bowl.

2. Place the ginger and whipping cream in a small saucepan.

3. Over medium heat, bring just barely to a boil. Pour into a bowl and let the mixture infuse for 30 minutes.

4. Strain the ginger cream back into a clean saucepan.

5. Over medium heat, bring the ginger cream barely to a boil.

6. Pour it over the chopped chocolate and let it sit for about a minute.

7. Whisk gently until it is completely smooth.

8. Add the corn syrup and butter and whisk gently until smooth to avoid bubbles.

9. Cool until it is almost room temperature but still warm enough to glaze the cake. It should be the consistency of paint.

BROWNIE aNGEL fOOD cake

YIELD: 8–10 SERVINGS

As a child, I always asked for an angel food cake with vanilla ice cream, fudge sauce and fresh strawberries for my birthday. Looking back, I can't fathom why I'd want such a bland cake. Determined to "brownie it up," I thought long and hard about the logistics of making a moist angel food cake with rich chocolate flavor; I didn't want the egg whites to collapse, but I wanted to make sure I got enough chocolate flavor. Here's the result: I used the recipe for Angel Food Cake by Flo Braker in *The Baker's Dozen Cookbook,* and added a little brownie magic. I hope Flo will forgive me for tinkering with her wonderful recipe.

1 ¼ cups	315 mL	**Classic Brownie batter (page 42), room temperature**
1 ½ cups	180 g	**icing sugar**
1 cup	120 g	**cake flour**
1 ½ cups	375 mL	**egg whites at room temperature**
½ tsp	2 mL	**salt**
1 ½ tsp	7 mL	**cream of tartar**
1 cup	200 g	**granulated sugar**
		icing sugar for dusting
		cocoa for dusting
2 pints	300 g	**fresh strawberries, sliced**
1 Tbsp	15 mL	**granulated sugar**
1 Tbsp	15 mL	**lemon juice**
1 cup	250 mL	**Chocolate Fudge Sauce (page 34)**

1. Preheat the oven to 350°F (180°C). Have ready an ungreased, 10-inch (4-L) tube pan with removable bottom.

2. If you have just made your brownie batter, it will be fluid. If you have refrigerated it, warm it in the microwave on defrost for about 3 minutes or until it is pourable. Stir to make sure it is fluid. Set aside.

3. Sift the icing sugar and cake flour together three times. Set aside.

4. Place the egg whites and salt in the bowl of an electric mixer fitted with the whisk attachment, and beat on medium speed until you see a layer of small bubbles. Add the cream of tartar.

5. Increase the speed until soft peaks form.

6. Gradually pour in the 1 cup (200 g) granulated sugar and beat only until soft, droopy peaks form.

7. With the mixer on low speed, gradually pour in 1 cup (250 mL) of the brownie batter. Increase the speed to medium for a few seconds only. You don't want to deflate the egg whites more than necessary.

8. Turn off the mixer, remove the bowl and scrape the batter on the whisk into the bowl.

9. Sprinkle ⅓ of the flour mixture over the top of the chocolate mixture and fold in gently, using a balloon whisk if possible, or a rubber spatula. Work gently but quickly to incorporate the remaining flour.

10. Pour half of the angel food batter into the pan. Jiggle gently to make it settle evenly.

11. Dip the tines of a fork into the remaining brownie batter and drizzle evenly over the batter in the pan. Use up about ½ of the remaining brownie batter, saving the rest for the top.

12. Top with the remaining angel food cake batter and drizzle the remaining brownie batter over the top. Don't worry if some of it starts to sink.

13. Bake for about 50 minutes or until it no longer looks moist and a toothpick comes out clean.

14. Invert the pan, or place on the neck of a tall bottle if your pan doesn't have "feet." Cool completely.

15. Run a knife around the outside edges and around the neck of the pan, as well as between the pan and the bottom of the cake, to release easily.

16. Invert the cake onto a serving dish. Dust with icing sugar and cocoa.

17. While the cake is cooling, mix the strawberries with the 1 Tbsp (15 mL) granulated sugar and lemon juice. Serve on the side of each slice, and drizzle with Chocolate Fudge Sauce.

not so wacky brownie cake*

with balsamic vinegar and marinated strawberries

YIELD: 10–12 SLICES

This is a recipe I found years ago and made for all my customers who wanted no-cholesterol and/or non-dairy cakes. When I first made this recipe, I didn't know about balsamic vinegar and grapeseed oil, which make all the difference in the world. In Italy, strawberries are served drizzled with balsamic vinegar, so it's an easy leap to use marinated strawberries as an accompaniment. Add something white, like whipped cream, ice cream or mascarpone cheese, and your plate will dazzle both the eye and the palate.

*I thought I was so clever using this name until I noticed that Michele Urvater, in her book *Chocolate Cake,* uses it for a similar recipe.

1 pint	150 g	fresh strawberries
1 Tbsp	15 mL	balsamic vinegar
		sugar to coat
3 cups	390 g	instant (see page 42) or all-purpose flour
2 cups	440 g	brown sugar
⅔ cup	80 g	cocoa
¼ tsp	1 mL	ground cinnamon
2 tsp	10 mL	baking soda
¼ tsp	1 mL	salt
2 cups	500 mL	water or strong brewed coffee
½ cup	125 mL	grapeseed or vegetable oil
2 Tbsp	30 mL	balsamic vinegar
7 oz	195 g	bittersweet chocolate, chopped
		icing sugar for dusting

1. Remove the stem ends from the strawberries and cut in half. Place in a bowl and sprinkle lightly with balsamic vinegar and sugar, just enough to barely coat them. Marinate in the fridge while you prepare the cake.

2. Preheat the oven to 350°F (180°C). Grease two 8- x 8-inch (20- x 20-cm) round pans with vegetable spray.

3. Place the flour, sugar, cocoa, cinnamon, baking soda and salt in the bowl of a food processor fitted with the steel blade.

4. Whisk the water or coffee, oil and vinegar together in a large pitcher.

5. Pulse the processor to mix the dry ingredients.

6. With the motor running, pour the wet ingredients through the feed tube to blend with the dry ingredients for about 5 seconds. Stop processing and scrape down the sides. Process for an additional 5 seconds.

7. Add the chopped chocolate to the bowl of the processor. Process for 5 additional seconds. (You can make the batter to this point and store it in the fridge for up to a week.)

8. Divide the batter between the prepared pans and bake until they spring back when pressed in the center, about 35–40 minutes.

9. Dust one layer with icing sugar and serve with the strawberries. Wrap the second layer in plastic and refrigerate, or wrap in foil and freeze.

Brownie points

This recipe is vegan, which means there are no animal ingredients such as eggs, milk or cheese. So it's a perfect dessert for lactose-intolerant as well as kosher or vegan guests. To glaze the cake and keep it vegan, use soy ganache. Simply substitute plain soy milk for the cream in the Ganache recipe (page 28).

Brownie cream cheese cupcakes

Mix 8 oz (112 g) cream cheese with ¼ cup (50 g) sugar and 2 eggs. Add ¼ cup (45 g) tiny chocolate chips or finely chopped chocolate. Fill greased muffin tins ¾ full with Not So Wacky Brownie Cake batter. Top with a tablespoon (15 mL) of the cream cheese mixture and bake at 350°F (180°C) until puffed. This is one of my favorite and most popular recipes.

Not so wacky fudge layer cake

You will need 2½ cups (625 mL) cooled Brownie Curd (page 24). Flip over one of the layer cakes and place on a serving dish. Spread with ½ cup (125 mL) of the curd. Place the second layer, bottom side up, on top. Spread the remaining curd thinly on the top and the sides. Refrigerate until the curd is set. Gently heat 1 recipe Shiny Chocolate Glaze (page 19) so it is barely warm and pourable. Set the cake on a rack set over a parchment-lined baking pan. Pour the glaze slowly over the center of the cake. Use a spatula, barely touching the glaze, to push it toward and down the sides. (If the glaze is too hot, it won't stick to the sides. If it doesn't, pick up the rack with the cake on it, and set on another piece of parchment paper. Pour the collected glaze on the pan over the cake again, making sure that it's not too cold or it will set in the middle and you won't be able to spread it at all.) The less you touch it with a spatula, the shinier it will be.

A delicious variation is to substitute 2½ cups (625 mL) of lightly sweetened whipped cream for the Brownie Curd between the layers. Glaze as above or with Ganache (page 28).

raspberry meringue molten chocolate cake

YIELD: 10 SERVINGS

After I submitted the manuscript for this book, I couldn't stop thinking about variations using the Not So Wacky Brownie Cake recipe. One day, finding some egg whites in my fridge and rummaging around for some frozen raspberries, I hit upon a new cake. Try it! You'll want to lick the bottom of the pan!

3 cups	750 mL	**Not So Wacky Cake batter (page 88) (about ½ recipe)**
2 pints	300 g	**raspberries, fresh or frozen**
5		**egg whites**
		pinch cream of tartar or drop of lemon juice
½ cup	100 g	**sugar**

1. Preheat the oven to 350°F (180°C). Grease a 9-inch (2.5-L) springform pan with vegetable spray. Line the bottom with a round of parchment paper, so you can easily slide the cake onto a serving platter. With its molten center, it will collapse if you try to move it any other way

2. Pour the batter into the prepared pan. Spread evenly with a spatula. It will not be much more than ¾ inch (2 cm) thick.

3. Sprinkle the raspberries evenly over the top of the batter, gently pressing them in so that they stick.

4. In the bowl of an electric mixer fitted with the whisk attachment, whip the egg whites until foamy. Add the cream of tartar or lemon juice.

5. Whisk until soft peaks form. Gradually add the sugar in a slow but steady stream.

6. Whisk until you have stiff peaks and the sugar is dissolved.

7. Drop the meringue in billows on top of the brownie batter. Keep it wispy or smooth the top, it's up to you. The layer will be generous.

8. Bake for about 35 minutes if you want a molten center, another 10 minutes if you don't. The meringue will rise nicely, but keep an eye on it so that it doesn't get too dark. If it does, turn the oven down to 300°F (150°C) and bake until done.

9. Remove from the oven and let cool for about 10 minutes before serving.

10. Remove the outer ring from the pan. Slide a spatula underneath the parchment paper and carefully move the cake onto a serving platter.

BROWNIE POINT

For individual servings, grease espresso cups well with vegetable spray. Fill the cups ⅔ full with cake batter. Top each with a few fresh or frozen raspberries and a dollop or swirl of meringue, about 2 inches (5 cm) above the rim of the pan. Bake at 300°F (150°C) for about 10 minutes, watching carefully that the meringue doesn't overbrown. If it starts to get too brown, remove from the oven immediately. Dust with icing sugar and serve immediately.

kentucky queen cake

YIELD: 8 SERVINGS

Sometimes all you want is a delicious little chocolate cake without too much fuss. This is definitely it.

6 oz	170 g	**bittersweet chocolate**
10 Tbsp	140 g	**butter**
3 Tbsp	45 mL	**bourbon**
⅛ tsp	0.5 mL	**kosher salt**
2 ½ oz	70 g	**toasted pecans**
2 Tbsp	30 mL	**all-purpose flour**
4		**eggs at room temperature, separated**
¼ cup	55 g	**brown sugar**
⅛ tsp	0.5 mL	**cream of tartar**
¾ cup	150 g	**granulated sugar**
		icing sugar for dusting

1. Preheat the oven to 350°F (180°C). Butter an 8-inch (20-cm) round pan and line the bottom with parchment paper.

2. Melt the chocolate and butter over low heat in a medium saucepan.

3. Add the bourbon and salt and stir to combine. Remove from the heat.

4. Place the pecans and flour in the bowl of a food processor. Process until they are finely chopped.

5. Whisk the egg yolks and brown sugar together and stir into the cooled chocolate mixture.

6. Stir the floured pecans into the chocolate mixture.

7. Using an electric mixer, whip the egg whites on low speed until frothy. Add the cream of tartar.

8. When soft peaks form, gradually add the granulated sugar. Beat until the whites are stiff but not dry.

9. Fold about ⅓ of the whites into the chocolate mixture to lighten it.

10. Fold the remaining whites into the mixture until only a few specks of white remain.

11. Pour into the prepared pan and bake until slightly puffed but no longer jiggly in the center, about 25–30 minutes.

12. Cool. Dust with icing sugar and don't forget to serve with vanilla ice cream!

Lemon marble stack cake

YIELD: 8–10 SERVINGS

This is one of those cakes in which mixing the components together would ruin each one, but stacking them allows each to shine. The basic lemon cake recipe and cold oven technique come from a cookbook by Edna Lewis and Scott Peacock, *The Gift of Southern Cooking*. I have, however, modified it slightly. By itself or enhanced with brownie batter, the cake is one you'll make over and over again. You'll only use half of the lemon cake batter for this presentation. You can bake the remaining batter in another loaf pan for plain lemon cake, or you can halve the recipe. The cakes freeze very well, wrapped in plastic and foil.

cake:

1 cup	227 g	**cold butter**
1 ⅔ cups	335 g	**sugar**
¼ tsp	1 mL	**kosher salt**
5		**eggs at room temperature**
2 ¼ cups	225 g	**sifted cake flour**
1 Tbsp	15 mL	**vanilla extract**
1 Tbsp	15 mL	**lemon juice**
		zest of 1 lemon
1 cup	250 mL	**Classic Brownie batter (page 42), warm**

1. Do not preheat the oven! Grease an 8- x 4-inch (1.5-L) loaf pan with vegetable spray. Line the bottom with overhanging parchment paper.

2. Place the butter in the bowl of an electric mixer fitted with the paddle attachment and beat for about 5 minutes or until waxy and shiny.

3. With the mixer on low speed, gradually add the sugar and salt. Scrape the sides and bottom of the bowl often. Increase the speed to medium and beat for about 5 minutes or until light and fluffy. The mixture will turn white.

4. Add the first 3 eggs one at a time, beating and scraping the sides after each addition.

5. After the third egg, add 2 Tbsp (30 mL) of the flour so that the batter doesn't separate. If you forget this step, don't worry, it will come back together again when all the flour is added.

6. Add the remaining eggs one at a time, as above.

7. Scrape the sides and bottom of the bowl.

8. Remove the bowl and beater from the mixer. Scrape off any dough sticking to the beater.

9. Mix in the remaining flour gently by hand using a rubber spatula. This ensures a more delicate cake.

10. Finally, add the vanilla, lemon juice and lemon zest.

11. Pour the brownie batter into the bottom of the prepared pan and smooth the top.

12. Pour half the lemon cake batter on top of the brownie batter and smooth to make it even. Place the remainder of the lemon cake batter in a second loaf pan, or fill greased muffin tins with it, and bake as follows.

13. Place the pan in the cold oven. Turn the oven to 225°F (105°C) and bake for 20 minutes.

14. Increase the temperature to 300°F (150°C) and bake for an additional 20 minutes.

15. Finally, set the temperature to 325°F (160°C) and bake for 20–30 minutes or until a toothpick comes out clean.

16. Remove from the oven and cool on a rack. Run a knife around the edges after 5 or 10 minutes and unmold the cake onto the rack.

17. Make the glaze while the cake cools, and brush it on while the cake is still warm.

ɢLaze:

⅓ cup	75 mL	**freshly squeezed lemon juice**
½ cup	100 g	**sugar**
1 Tbsp	15 mL	**butter**
⅛ tsp	0.5 mL	**kosher salt**

1. Place all the ingredients in a small non-reactive saucepan. Stir over medium heat until the sugar is just dissolved.

2. Brush the glaze over the top and sides of the warm cake.

BROWNIE POINT

To vary this presentation, use both batters to make a marble cake. Pour ⅔ of the lemon cake batter into the pan. Top with the brownie batter. Complete with the remaining lemon batter. Insert a thin knife ¾ of the way down into the batter and zigzag around the pan. You won't see the marbling effect until the cake is fully baked and sliced.

fLourLess chocoLate cake

YIELD: 12 GENEROUS SERVINGS

This was formerly known as Fallen Soufflé Cake because it would rise in the oven and collapse when cool, leaving a higher edge and a cracked crust frequently hidden under a light sprinkling of icing sugar. It wasn't bad. It just didn't reach its potential until I stumbled on a new technique. If you make and bake this the same day, the cake will rise and then settle somewhat, but if you prepare the batter the day before, chill it in the fridge overnight, and then bake it, the result will be, for some reason I can't figure out, a cake that doesn't settle as much, with a light, custardy, but definitely fudgy consistency. If possible, eat it while still warm. It's incredible.

1 pound	454 g	**bittersweet chocolate, chopped**
1 cup	227 g	**cold butter, cubed**
½ cup	100 g	**sugar**
6		**eggs**
1 Tbsp	15 mL	**Kahlua or brewed coffee**
½ tsp	2 mL	**salt**
2 cups	500 mL	**whipped cream**

1. Place a 10-inch-square (25-cm) piece of parchment paper over the bottom of a 9-inch (2.5-L) springform pan. Fit the exterior ring over the base and close. This should create a waterproof barrier. If you are in doubt, wrap the bottom of the pan in foil that goes ¾ of the way up the outside. Grease the pan with vegetable spray.

2. Melt the chocolate and butter in a saucepan over low heat.

3. When the chocolate, but not all of the butter, is melted, remove the bowl from the heat and allow the heat of the chocolate to melt the remaining butter. Stir to blend well. Let cool a bit. Set aside.

4. Place the sugar and eggs in the bowl of an electric mixer and fit with the whisk attachment. Beat on high speed for about 5 minutes or until light and triple in volume.

5. Turn the mixer to the lowest speed and pour in the chocolate mixture. Continue to mix until the chocolate is completely incorporated.

6. Add the Kahlua or coffee and salt.

7. Pour the batter into the prepared pan. At this point, you can either bake the cake following the instructions in step 10 or cover the pan tightly with plastic wrap and refrigerate for 8 hours or overnight.

8. When you are ready to bake the cake, preheat the oven to 300°F (150°C). Boil about 4 cups (1 L) of water.

9. Place the cake batter in the prepared cake pan, then place this pan in a roasting pan in the oven. Fill the roasting pan with enough boiling water to reach ¾ up the sides of the cake pan.

10. Bake for about 35 minutes or until the cake is slightly puffed. If it puffs and cracks, it's okay. The center should be slightly jiggly. It will continue to cook when removed from the oven and will completely firm up in the fridge.

11. Remove from the oven and let sit in the hot water for another 15 minutes.

12. Remove from the water and let cool for 30 minutes. It will still be warm in the center.

13. Place the cake on a plate and remove the exterior ring. Place a second plate lightly on top and turn the cake upside down, being careful not to squeeze the cake while doing so.

14. Remove the plate and then the metal bottom, and peel off the parchment paper. Place the plate on the bottom of the cake and turn right side up.

15. At this point, you may serve the cake, which will be custardy in the center and won't slice perfectly (but boy, oh boy, will it taste good), or you can chill it completely. (If serving chilled, refrigerate it in the pan once it has cooled. This will make unmolding it a lot easier.)

16. Slice it as you would a cheesecake, by immersing a knife in hot water and wiping it dry before every slice. Serve with a dollop of whipped cream.

BROWNIE POINT

Lava Cake, Molten Chocolate Cake, Oozy to the Core Brownie Cake. Call it what you will, this recipe lends itself perfectly to the very trendy soft-core chocolate cake. Make the recipe above and pour it into greased ramekins. Place them in a hot water bath reaching halfway up the sides of the ramekins, and bake until slightly puffed, about 15 minutes. Remove from the oven and let sit in the hot water for another 5 minutes. Remove ramekins from the water and let sit for an additional 5–10 minutes before unmolding onto a plate. Use a knife to loosen the edges. The exterior will be pudding-like, while the interior will be jiggly to completely oozy. Utter decadence!

CHOCOLate BROWNIe CRUMB Cake

YIELD: 16 SERVINGS

My all-time favorite New York City specialty is crumb cake. All over the city, bakeries produce this great, simple cake from scratch. It's not always good, but in the Chelsea Market there's a bakery that makes the best there is. Its crumb layer is a good two times the height of the cake layer. The crumbs are pea-sized and crispy crunchy without being too tough or too sweet. The cake layer is a moist golden yellow cake, also not too sweet or too bland. An apple version that adds cinnamon to the crumbs and sautéed apples to the top of the cake below the crumbs just knocks my socks off. So, naturally, when thinking, nay dreaming, of a better version, I decided to make a chocolate brownie rendition. As I was editing this book, I visited the Chelsea Market and to my delight they had read my mind: what was missing was a chocolate crumb cake, and now they have it. Here's my version that's pretty darn close to the original.

1 recipe		Brownie Crumble (page 38) made with ¼ tsp freshly grated nutmeg added with flour
1 ½ cups	195 g	all-purpose flour
½ cup	60 g	cocoa
1 tsp	5 mL	baking soda
½ tsp	2 mL	baking powder
¼ tsp	1 mL	freshly ground nutmeg
½ tsp	2 mL	salt
8 Tbsp	115 g	butter, slightly softened
1 cup	200 g	sugar
¼ cup	55 g	brown sugar
2		eggs, room temperature
1 cup	250 mL	sour cream
1 tsp	5 mL	vanilla
		icing sugar
		Ganache (page 28) (optional)

1. Preheat the oven to 350°F (180°C). Line a 9- x 9-inch (23- x 23-cm) square pan or an 8-inch (20-cm) round tube pan with parchment paper, greasing sides and bottom with vegetable spray.

2. Make the Brownie Crumble and set aside.

3. Mix all the dry ingredients in a bowl and set aside.

4. In the bowl of an electric mixer, beat the butter until soft, scraping the sides and bottom occasionally.

5. Add both sugars and beat on medium speed until light and fluffy, about 10 minutes, scraping the bowl often.

6. Add the eggs one at a time, scraping the bowl after each addition and beating until fully incorporated.

7. Mix the sour cream with the vanilla.

8. Alternately add the dry ingredients with the sour cream. Mix on low and turn off the mixer before the last of the flour is fully incorporated.

9. Use a rubber spatula to finish the mixing, gently folding in whatever flour remains visible.

10. Pour and spread the batter evenly in the prepared pan.

11. Sprinkle the crumble evenly over the top.

12. Bake for about 30–40 minutes, until the center begins to dome, being watchful that the crumble doesn't get too dark around the edges. If this happens, cover the crumble loosely with foil. I bake the cake until the center is even with the sides so that, when it cools, the center is a bit moister than the sides. Try it this way first and adjust the baking time to your preference.

13. When cool, dust with icing sugar and/or drizzle with Ganache.

BROWNIE POINT

This recipe makes awesome muffins as well. Just scoop and press crumble gently into the batter (the crumbs tend to fall off). Bigger muffins are better than mini, as the batter dries out more quickly the smaller they are.

chocolate espresso coffee cake

YIELD: 10–12 SERVINGS

I developed this cake for a wonderful new bundt pan with a terraced pattern. It got me thinking about chocolate glaze wending its way down the sides of the cake in a kind of circular pattern rather than its usual downward drip. It took me many tries to get the texture just right without compromising the deep, rich chocolate flavor. This cake can be made into one big bundt or two 9-inch (23-cm) cake layers for the fabulous chocolate layer cake in the Brownie Point.

2 ¼ cups	300 g	all-purpose flour
1 tsp	5 mL	baking soda
1 ¼ tsp	6 mL	baking powder
½ tsp	2 mL	kosher salt
8 Tbsp	115 g	butter, at room temperature
½ cup	100 g	granulated sugar
1 cup	220 g	brown sugar
½ cup	125 mL	butter, melted
½ cup	60 g	cocoa
1 Tbsp	15 mL	freshly ground espresso powder
3		eggs
1 cup	250 mL	brewed coffee
1 cup	175 g	chocolate chips
1 cup	250 mL	Mocha Ganache

1. Preheat the oven to 350°F (180°C). Grease a 10-cup (2.5-L) bundt pan.

2. Whisk together the flour, baking soda, baking powder and salt. Set aside.

3. Beat the room-temperature butter in the bowl of an electric mixer until light, about 5 minutes.

4. Add both sugars and beat on medium speed for an additional 10 minutes, until the butter and sugar are very light and airy. Scrape the sides and bottom of the bowl from time to time.

5. While the butter is beating, pour the melted butter over the cocoa to hydrate it. Mix into a smooth paste. Add the espresso powder and mix to blend. Set aside.

6. Reduce the mixer speed to low. Add the eggs one at a time, incorporating each completely before adding the next one. Scrape the sides and bottom after the second egg.

7. Turn the mixer to high for 30 seconds then turn it to low. Add the cocoa mixture. Mix for one minute, then scrape the sides and bottom of the bowl.

mocha ganache:

YIELD: SCANT 2 CUPS (500 mL)

8 oz	227 g	**bittersweet chocolate, chopped**
1 cup	250 mL	**heavy cream**
2 Tbsp	30 mL	**freshly ground espresso powder**

8. Mix again for 1 minute.

9. Add the flour mixture alternately with the coffee while mixing on low speed. Turn the mixer off before all the flour is incorporated.

10. Remove the bowl from the mixer. Use a rubber spatula to fold in the remaining flour, being gentle and careful to mix in any unblended batter from the sides and bottom.

11. When completely smooth, gently fold in the chocolate chips.

12. Pour into the prepared pan and bake for about 45–50 minutes or until firm but resilient to the touch (you will hear a slow popping of bubbles when you put your ear close to the surface of the cake).

13. Remove from the oven and let sit in the pan to firm up for about 30 minutes.

14. Unmold and serve with Mocha Ganache (or serve as is dusted with icing sugar).

1. Place the chocolate in a medium-sized bowl.

2. Heat the cream in a small saucepan over medium heat.

3. When you see bubbles around the edges, stir in the espresso powder.

4. Just before the cream comes to a boil, remove it from the heat and let it steep for 30 minutes.

5. Return the pan to the heat and bring it to just below a boil.

6. Pour it over the chocolate and let sit for 5 minutes.

7. Whisk it gently until completely smooth.

8. Let it thicken, stirring occasionally to get it to the point where it will wend its way down and around the cake and cling to the sides in thick dribbles, rather than in thin, skimpy streaks. Have patience. The consistency should be that of paint: thick but creamy and still flowing, about 80–85°F (27–30°C).

9. Pour over the cake and let gravity do the work!

BROWNIE POINT

To make this into a layer cake, grease 2 9-inch (23-cm) baking pans with vegetable spray. Preheat the oven to 350°F (180°C). Make the batter and divide between the pans. Bake until a toothpick comes out clean. Cool the layers completely. Meanwhile, make a double batch of the ganache recipe and let it thicken about an hour or so in the fridge, until it has the consistency of sour cream. Slice each cake layer in half horizontally so that you have four layers and spread each layer with ⅕ of the ganache, reserving what's left for the sides and top. Press the top of the cake gently. Spread any frosting that has oozed out the sides around the edges to seal any crumbs. Chill for 15 minutes. Remove from the fridge and frost the top and sides with the remaining ganache.

banana brownie muffin cakes
YIELD: 24 MINI MUFFINS

There's a blurry line that divides cupcakes and muffins but, quite honestly, who cares as long as they're good? Here's a recipe that's quick and easy to assemble and is as much at home at breakfast as it is ending an elegant dinner. Garnished with a tumble of raspberries, these little gems are two-bite perfection. They're moist and tender, with just a hint of banana. Best of all, you can assemble them in just under 10 minutes.

1 cup	130 g	all-purpose flour
½ cup	60 g	cocoa
1 cup	200 g	sugar
¾ tsp	3 mL	baking powder
¼ tsp	1 mL	baking soda
¾ tsp	3 mL	salt
1	85 g	small banana, peeled
2		eggs
¾ cup	175 mL	milk
4 Tbsp	60 mL	melted butter
2 tsp	10 mL	vanilla
5 oz	140 g	finely chopped chocolate or mini chocolate chips
1 cup	250 mL	Ganache (page 28)

1. Preheat the oven to 375°F (190°C). Spray vegetable spray inside muffin tin or line with paper liners.

2. Whisk together the flour, cocoa, sugar, baking powder, baking soda and salt. Set aside.

3. In the bowl of a food processor blend the banana, eggs, milk, melted butter and vanilla.

4. Add the dry ingredients and pulse until just blended, scraping the sides to incorporate all the ingredients.

5. Add the chocolate and process a second or two to incorporate.

6. Use an ice cream scoop to portion the batter into the prepared pan.

7. Bake about 18 minutes until the muffins are domed and bounce back when pressed gently.

8. Let cool and dip the tops in barely warmed Ganache.

BROWNIE POINT

If you prefer cake to cupcakes, simply grease an 8-inch (20-cm) bundt pan and fill it with batter. Bake at 350°F (180°C) for 30-40 minutes or until a toothpick comes out with a few crumbs clinging to it. Cool for 20 minutes in the pan before unmolding. Glaze with Ganache when cake has reached room temperature.

Cookies with Crunch

4

ultimate, ultimate chocolate chunk cookies

YIELD: **18** BIG COOKIES

Everyone calls their chocolate chunk cookies "the ultimate," but mine are the real deal. How do I know? I brought these into work one day to get a reaction from some of the most critical, best-informed food people I know and they all raved about them! Once you make them, you won't turn back to those imposters! Oat flour is found in natural food stores or in the natural food section of many supermarkets. If you can't find it, pulse rolled oats to a fine powder in the food processor.

2 oz	56 g	**walnuts, coarsely chopped**
2 oz	56 g	**pecans, coarsely chopped**
½ cup	50 g	**coconut**
½ cup	45 g	**rolled oats (not instant)**
1 cup	130 g	**all-purpose flour**
½ cup	55 g	**oat flour**
¾ tsp	3 mL	**baking soda**
½ tsp	2 mL	**kosher salt**
¼ tsp	1 mL	**ground cinnamon**
12 Tbsp	165 g	**butter**
¾ cup	160 g	**brown sugar**
¾ cup less 1 Tbsp	140 g	**granulated sugar**
2		**eggs**
1 tsp	5 mL	**vanilla extract**
12 oz	335 g	**milk chocolate, chopped into chip-sized pieces**
12 oz	335 g	**bittersweet chocolate, chopped into chip-sized pieces**

1. Preheat the oven to 350°F (180°C).

2. Place the walnuts and pecans on a cookie sheet and toast for 12 minutes.

3. Place the coconut and rolled oats on a separate cookie sheet and toast for about 10 minutes, tossing occasionally until just golden brown. Don't overbake. Set the nuts and coconut mixture aside.

4. Mix the flour, oat flour, baking soda, baking powder, salt and cinnamon in a medium bowl.

5. In the bowl of an electric mixer beat the butter until soft, about 2 minutes.

6. Add both sugars and blend for an additional 2 minutes, scraping the sides and bottom of the bowl once or twice.

7. Add the eggs one at a time, scraping the bowl between additions.

8. Add the vanilla and mix briefly.

9. Add the dry ingredients and mix just until barely blended.

10. Add the nuts and coconut mixture. Mix for about 1 minute.

11. Remove the bowl from the mixer and add both chocolates, folding them into the batter with a rubber spatula.

12. Use a 3-oz (85-g) scoop to portion the cookies 3 inches (8 cm) apart on a cookie sheet.

13. Bake for 10–12 minutes, or until the cookies are golden and firm around the edges but still a bit soft in the center.

14. Let them cool slightly before removing from the baking sheet onto a cooling rack.

BROWNIE TRISCOTTI

YIELD: **30 TRISCOTTI**

The world of cooking is filled with classic ways to use up leftovers—think chef salad, soup and quiche. When professional bakers get together, the conversation frequently revolves around what to do with leftovers and crumbs. Whether it's cake trimmings or muffins that didn't sell, we all want to use rather than throw them out. Rum balls, bran muffins, and yes, even brownies are frequent recipients of these bakery orphans, in no way detracting from their taste but certainly expanding the recipe to yield more. Thus, it wasn't surprising to me to find a recipe in Nancy Silverton's *Pastries from La Brea Bakery* that reuses cookie crumbs. She asks the question: What would you call a cookie that's been baked three times?" meaning a cookie that includes crumbs that have already been baked and then baked twice more? I call them Triscotti. With this recipe, based on hers, you can use chocolate muffin or cornbread crumbs; you can add nuts or leave them out; you can even change the spices. In short, they're extremely versatile, quick and very delicious.

½ cup + 1 Tbsp	60 g	**oatmeal**
½ cup + 1 Tbsp	60 g	**coconut**
2 cups	225 g	**chocolate cake, muffin, brownie or cookie crumbs, dried crisp in a low-heat oven about 15–20 minutes, stirring from time to time**
1 ¼ cups	165 g	**all-purpose flour**
¾ cup	135g	**brown sugar**
1 tsp	5 mL	**baking powder**
1 tsp	5 mL	**baking soda**
½ tsp	2 mL	**kosher salt**
¾ tsp	3 mL	**cinnamon**
½ tsp	2 mL	**ginger**
½ tsp	2 mL	**cardamom**
2		**eggs**
1		**egg yolk**
3 Tbsp	45 mL	**melted butter**
3 oz	100 g	**bittersweet chocolate, finely chopped**
3 oz	100 g	**nuts (optional)**
1 cup	200 g	**cinnamon sugar**

1. Preheat oven to 350°F (180°C). Line two cookie sheets with parchment paper or Silpat.

2. Mix the oatmeal and coconut together and spread on one of the cookie sheets. Bake in the oven about 10 minutes, stirring occasionally until they are a nice golden brown and release their aroma. Cool.

3. In the bowl of a food processor, process the crumbs until they are even in size.

4. Add the flour, sugar, baking powder, baking soda, salt and spices and process until blended.

5. In a small bowl, mix together the eggs, yolk and melted butter. With the machine running, pour into the processor feed tube.

6. Blend just until it forms a thick, sticky dough.

7. Remove the lid of the processor and sprinkle the chocolate and the nuts over the top of the dough. Scrape the sides while you're at it.

8. Pulse about 10 times, until the nuts and chocolate are barely incorporated. Add the toasted oatmeal and coconut and pulse briefly to blend.

9. Wet your hands with cold water. Divide the dough between the two baking sheets. Pat it into two flattened logs about 12 inches long x 3 inches wide (30 x 8 cm).

10. Sprinkle the top of each with cinnamon sugar.

11. Bake for 30 minutes or until the logs are firm to the touch.

12. Remove and cool for five minutes.

13. Turn the oven down to 300°F (150°C).

14. Using a serrated knife, slice each log into 25 biscotti.

15. Place them cut side down on the baking sheets. Sprinkle cinnamon sugar over all of them. Turn them over and sprinkle the other side.

16. Return to the oven for an additional 25-30 minutes or until they are crisp. Be sure not to overbake as they will burn.

17. Store in a tightly sealed jar at room temperature or freeze.

shortbread
chocolate crunch cookies

YIELD: 48 COOKIES, PLUS LEFTOVER CHOCOLATE ALMOND BRITTLE

Why is it that during the holidays, when we have less time, we take on new projects? Take heart, shortbread is a seasonal favorite, beloved by everyone and very easy to make. Chocolate nut brittle is also a favorite and very simple as long as you have a basic candy thermometer…in fact, it's so good and easy that if you don't have a candy thermometer, it's worth getting one. This recipe, or project, is two in one, allowing you to actually make three different holiday items, plain shortbread cookies, Chocolate Almond Brittle, and the Shortbread Chocolate Crunch Cookies, all perfect for gift-giving. Spread over two baking sessions on different days, and it's a breeze. Not a project after all, but pure pleasure. Just remember to make the brittle first so the warm cookies can melt the chocolate, enabling the brittle to stick on top.

chocolate almond brittle:

1 cup	227 g	**butter**
1 ½ cups	300 g	**sugar**
3 Tbsp	45 mL	**corn syrup**
3 Tbsp	45 mL	**water**
8 oz	225 g	**unblanched almonds, toasted, and finely chopped, divided**
12 oz	335 g	**bittersweet chocolate, chopped**
		kosher salt for sprinkling

1. Butter the bottom of an 11- x 17-inch (28- x 44-cm) jelly roll pan.

2. In a high-sided, medium saucepan, melt the butter over medium heat.

3. Place the sugar in a bowl. Mix the corn syrup and water together and pour over the sugar. Mix to moisten the sugar.

4. When the butter is fully melted, remove from the heat and add the sugar mixture.

5. Return to medium-high heat. Clip on a candy thermometer. As the mixture boils and becomes thicker and thicker, stir from time to time to clear the sides and bottom.

6. When the thermometer registers 300°F (150°C), remove the pot from the heat and stir in half the almonds. Mix gently to assure that the almonds don't sink to the bottom.

7. Pour the candy into the prepared baking pan and use a spatula to gently push it to the edges. Work quickly because it will begin to harden.

8. Let sit until firm, about 20 minutes. It will still be hot but cool enough to turn onto a cutting board.

9. Use a paper towel to fully wipe off the butter from the surface of the candy.

10. Melt ¾ of the chocolate in a bowl over simmering water. Add the rest and stir gently until it is melted.

11. Pour half the chocolate over the brittle and spread with a spatula.

12. Working quickly, sprinkle half the remaining nuts evenly over the surface. Sprinkle lightly with salt.

13. Place a piece of parchment paper on top of the nut- and chocolate-covered brittle and place a baking sheet bottom side against the parchment. Holding both, flip the brittle over.

14. Pour the remaining chocolate over the brittle, spread the rest of the nuts over top and sprinkle lightly with salt. Let sit until the chocolate has cooled completely.

15. Store in a tightly covered container. Or place in pretty glass containers and give as impressive gifts.

SHORTBREAD COOKIES:

1 ¾ cups	230 g	**all-purpose flour**
½ cup	55 g	**rice flour**
½ tsp	2 mL	**kosher salt**
1 cup	227 g	**cold butter**
½ cup	100 g	**superfine sugar**
48		**½-inch (1-cm) Chocolate Almond Brittle pieces**

1. Preheat the oven to 300°F (150°C).

2. Sift the flour, rice flour and salt together. Set aside.

3. Cut the butter into 1-inch (3cm) pieces and place in the bowl of an electric mixer fitted with the paddle attachment. Mix for about 1 minute on medium speed or until it has softened and is no longer in pieces. Scrape the sides of the bowl.

4. Gradually add the sugar, a tablespoon at a time, mixing for no more than 2 minutes. Scrape the sides of the bowl.

5. Add half the flour mixture and blend on low speed for 1 minute, or until it is almost completely incorporated.

6. Remove the bowl from the mixer. Add the remaining flour and gently and quickly mix it into the butter mixture with your hands or a rubber spatula. Work quickly if you are using your hands, since you don't want to warm up the butter. It will feel a bit like pie dough. Don't overwork the dough. You want the cookies to melt in your mouth!

7. If the dough gets too soft, place in the fridge for about 15 minutes to allow it to firm up.

8. Using a small scoop or a teaspoon, plop rounded pieces of dough about 1/2 inch (1cm) apart on the baking sheet. Use your index finger to make an indentation in the center of each. Round any ragged edges with your fingertip. (Leave some with no indent if you want to make some plain shortbread cookies.)

9. You should have enough dough for three baking pans. If you can't bake them all at once, place the unused dough, or the formed dough on extra baking pans, in the fridge while the first pan bakes.

10. Bake for about 35 minutes or until barely brown.

11. Remove from the oven and immediately place a single piece of Chocolate Almond Brittle in the center of each cookie. Don't press down. The heat from the cookies will melt the chocolate and glue it to the surface.

12. Carefully place the finished cookies on a baking rack to cool completely.

13. Store in a sealed container for up to a month.

mILk cHocoLate
peanut Butter cruncH cookIes

YIELD: 24 COOKIES

These are absurdly good. How do I know? Because when I brought them to work, no one could stop eating them and people who are very picky wanted seconds and thirds! This is one of those recipes that soars from the use of milk chocolate. Don't overbake, as these cookies are fragile.

praLine cruncH:

3 ½ oz	105 g	**dry-roasted peanuts**
⅔ cup	140 g	**granulated sugar**

1. Place the peanuts in a 4-inch (10-cm) circle on a grease-resistant surface: parchment paper, Silpat or a greased cookie sheet.

2. Place the sugar in a medium saucepan over medium heat. The sugar will eventually melt and begin to caramelize. When it does, start swirling the pan to ensure that all the sugar melts. When it is a rich chestnut brown, quickly remove from the heat and pour over the peanuts, covering as much as you can. Set aside to cool.

cHocoLate swIrL:

2 Tbsp	30 mL	**butter, softened**
6 oz	170 g	**bittersweet chocolate**
1 oz	28 g	**unsweetened chocolate**
3 Tbsp	45 mL	**granulated sugar**
1		**egg**

1. Place all the ingredients in the same saucepan (you don't have to clean it). Melt over low heat, stirring so as not to burn the bottom.

2. Remove from the heat and let cool while you make the cookie batter.

3. Mix the egg into the cooled chocolate mixture.

cookie batter:

½ cup	125 mL	peanut butter
8 Tbsp	115 g	butter
¾ cup	115 g	brown sugar
¼ cup	50 g	granulated sugar
1		egg
¾ cup	95 g	all-purpose flour
¼ tsp	1 mL	baking soda
¼ tsp	1 mL	kosher salt
3 oz	105 g	dry-roasted peanuts
7 oz	195 g	milk chocolate, chopped

1. Preheat the oven to 350°F (180°C). Line 2 cookie sheets with parchment paper—the cookies are fragile and if they stick to the pan, removal will crumble them.

2. Place the peanut butter and butter in the bowl of an electric mixer fitted with the paddle attachment. Beat on low speed until entirely smooth and café au lait in color. Scrape the sides and bottom of the bowl to make sure all the butter is mixed in.

3. Add both sugars and mix until smooth, about 3 minutes.

4. Add the egg, beating until thoroughly mixed in.

5. Add the flour, baking soda and salt. Mix on low, just until completely blended.

6. Place the cooled praline disc on a chopping board and chop into pieces roughly the size of peas with a chef's knife. Don't worry if some are bigger or some smaller.

7. Add the chopped praline, peanuts and chopped milk chocolate to the batter. Mix with a rubber spatula to coat the chunky ingredients with dough.

8. Gently add the chocolate swirl mixture. Fold in to peanut butter batter gently. It doesn't have to be fully incorporated.

9. Use a small ice cream scoop or tablespoon to drop dough onto the prepared pans. Bake for about 12–14 minutes or until chewy-looking but not wet or stiff. They will look puffed and cracked on top.

10. Remove from the oven and cool completely on the pan until firm. Use a spatula to remove from the pan. These are fragile. If by some miracle you have some crumbs left, be sure to use them in your Brownie Truffles (page 156).

HaLvaH BROWNIE COOKIES

YIELD: 48 COOKIES

Sesame seeds aren't usually found with chocolate but I was determined to figure out something because I'm so fond of both ingredients. You can omit the diced apricots (or substitute raisins) but I have found that apricots enhance the shelf-life of the cookies and add a subtle zing, so try them at least once. Halvah can frequently be found in the candy section or specialty sections of grocery stores, and certainly in markets catering to Middle Eastern or Mediterranean communities.

12 ½ oz	350 g	halvah
5 ½ oz	155 g	bittersweet chocolate, chopped
1		egg
4 Tbsp	35 g	flour
¼ cup	55 g	brown sugar
⅛ tsp	0.5 mL	kosher salt
5 ½ oz	155 g	dried apricots, diced (about 20)

1. Preheat the oven to 350°F (180°C). Line two cookie sheets with parchment paper.

2. Place the halvah in the bowl of a food processor fitted with the steel blade. Process until the mixture is smooth.

3. Add the chocolate and process until the two are combined.

4. Add the egg and process until smooth.

5. Add the flour, brown sugar and salt. Process just until smooth.

6. Turn the mixture into a bowl and add the apricots. The dough will be fairly thick, but don't worry.

7. Use a teaspoon to scoop mounds of dough onto the cookie sheet, about 12 per pan.

8. Bake for about 12 minutes or until the cookies are just firm to the touch. Don't overbake them.

9. Place on a rack to cool.

BROWNIE POINT

You can enhance the sesame taste and add some additional crunch by rolling the dough into balls, dropping them into a bowl of sesame seeds and tossing to coat completely. Place on the cookie sheet and flatten into a fat disc with the palm of your hand. Bake as above. When cooled, you can eat them as is, or dip half in melted chocolate!

CHOCOLate BROWNIe CIGARS

YIELD: 6

French pastry sets the groundwork for so many possibilities. And much of it is very simple to do. Take the classic "cigarette cookie," for example. A simple recipe can be rolled into tubes and filled with whipped cream or lemon curd or folded over a cup and turned into perfect vessels for berries and ice cream. As delicious and sophisticated as this is, it can always be improved upon with the addition of some chocolate. So, instead of the classic cigarettes, I've created a new classic: cigars filled with chocolate curd. (Note to the reader: Sometimes these don't really look as much like cigars as unmentionables. I once served these at a catering. There was much laughter in the room as people ate them. As Freud might have said, "Sometimes a cigar is just a cigar.")

6		Tuile Cookies (page 112), rolled around a spoon handle to form a hollow tube
1 cup	250 mL	Brownie Curd (page 24), placed in a piping bag fitted with a small plain or star tip
6		fresh raspberries
		icing sugar for garnish

1. Pipe the Brownie Curd into the tube cookies, filling half from one end, then turning and filling from the other end.

2. Gently push a raspberry into one end to resemble the burning end of a cigar, and dust with icing sugar to suggest ash. Now you're smokin'!

BROWNIE tacos

YIELD: 6

These are elegant-but-fun plated desserts. Line up your plates and work like a professional, assembly-line fashion. This way, each dessert will be identical and it'll only take minutes to complete. The curd is easier to handle if placed in a piping tube. The optional queso fresco is a soft, fresh milk cheese that has a slightly sweet-and-salty edge, so it provides a nice contrast to the richness of the other ingredients. Although the tuile batter makes about 18 cookies, this recipe is for 6 tacos. Leftover batter can be frozen for up to 3 months.

tuile cookies:

2 ½ Tbsp	40 mL	**butter, softened**
½ cup	60 g	**icing sugar**
2		**egg whites at room temperature**
2 Tbsp	30 mL	**all-purpose flour**
2 Tbsp	30 mL	**cocoa, sifted**

1. Preheat the oven to 350°F (180°C). Line a baking sheet with parchment paper. You will need a scoop the size of a melon baller or a cereal spoon, a small offset spatula and a rolling pin for forming the cookies. Keep these near at hand.

2. Beat the butter in the bowl of an electric mixer on low speed until soft.

3. Add the sugar gradually, beating on medium to create a smooth paste. Scrape the sides and bottom of the bowl.

4. Whisk the egg whites gently to break them up, then add gradually to the batter. The butter mixture may curdle; this is okay.

5. Turn the mixer off and scrape the sides and bottom of the bowl.

6. Add the flour and cocoa. Mix on low speed, mixing only enough to blend. The batter with be thick enough to drop off the paddle in blobs. Let rest 30 minutes.

7. Using a scoop or cereal spoon, drop mounds of batter onto one of the prepared baking sheets. Until you have mastered the easy art of rolling the cookies, put only 3 mounds on a sheet.

8. Use your spatula to spread the dough into circles about 2 ½ inches (6 cm) in diameter, being careful not to create any holes or areas that are too thin.

9. Bake for approximately 8 minutes, or until the batter feels moist but firm to the gentle pressure of your finger.

10. Remove the pan from the oven and work quickly. Drape the pliable cookies over the rolling pin and press gently so they take its shape. When they are cool and completely firm, remove to a rack.

11. Repeat making 3 more cookies. As you get more experienced, you can put more cookies on the sheet. If the cookies get too firm to form, return briefly to the oven to soften.

12. Refrigerate or freeze unused batter.

BROWNIE tacos:

¾ cup	175 mL	**Brownie Curd (page 24), placed in a piping bag with a small plain or star tip**
¾ cup	175 mL	**crumbled-up brownies, cake or cookies**
½ pint	75 g	**crushed raspberries or strawberries**
10		**mint leaves, piled on top of one another, rolled and finely sliced crosswise (chiffonade)**
½ cup	50 g	**crumbled queso fresco (a soft, sweet fresh milk cheese) or 1 cup (250 mL) unsweetened whipped cream**

1. Lay out 6 plates and place a tuile, curved side down, on each plate. Pipe or spoon a squiggle of Brownie Curd down the center.

2. Top with crumbled brownie (chopped meat!).

3. Sprinkle with crushed raspberries (tomatoes!).

4. Sprinkle with mint (shredded lettuce!).

5. Top with crumbled queso fresco (cheese!) or whipped cream.

6. Serve within 30 minutes of assembly or the cookies may droop.

mom's crunch center cookies...
brownie version

YIELD: ABOUT 36 COOKIES

My mom all but threatened to disown me if I ever published her fabulous secret recipe, Crunch Center Cookies. (Just kidding, of course. Mom gives the recipe to anyone who asks.) So, I came up with this fabulous brownie version, basically a shortbread stuffed with praline and milk chocolate, then barely baked and rolled in icing sugar. Resist the temptation to overbake them. You want the centers slightly moist.

pecan praline:

1 cup	100 g	sugar
6 oz	180 g	pecan pieces

1. Spread the pecans in a circle about 8 inches (20 cm) in diameter on a heat-resistant surface—parchment paper, Silpat or a greased cookie sheet.

2. Place sugar in a small saucepan over medium heat and allow to melt. It will start on the outside edges. Swirl the pan to bring the cooked syrup in and the crystals out to the edges. (You may stir with a heat-resistant rubber spatula.) Cook until the sugar is completely melted and a deep golden brown. The syrup will be clear. Watch carefully and continuously as it can burn quickly.

3. Pour over the nuts so that all of them are fully or partially covered by caramel. Cool completely.

4. When cool, chop into coarse pieces. There will be a lot of caramel "dust" on the chopping board. Use all of it in the cookies.

cookie dough:

2 ⅓ cups	300 g	**all-purpose flour**
1 cup less 2 Tbsp	100 g	**cocoa**
1 tsp	5 mL	**kosher salt**
1 ½ cups	340 g	**cold butter**
2 tsp	10 mL	**vanilla**
¾ cup	165 g	**brown sugar**
1 recipe		**Pecan Praline, chopped**
6 oz	180 g	**milk chocolate, coarsely chopped**
1 cup	120 g	**icing sugar, sifted**

1. Preheat oven to 350°F (180°C). Line a cookie sheet with parchment paper or Silpat.

2. Mix together the flour, cocoa and salt. Set aside.

3. In the bowl of an electric mixer, beat the butter and vanilla until softened.

4. Add the brown sugar and beat on low speed until blended.

5. Add the flour mixture and blend until the dough comes together. It will be stiff.

6. Add the chopped praline. Some of it will not incorporate but will stay on the bottom of the bowl.

7. Add the chopped chocolate and mix briefly.

8. Remove the bowl from the mixer and, using your hands, lightly knead the dough to mix in any chunks of chocolate and praline that have resisted incorporation.

9. Place walnut-sized balls of dough on a cookie sheet using your hands to lightly roll them into rough rounds.

10. Bake for 10 minutes and remove from the oven. At this point, cookies are too fragile to remove from the pan.

11. Cool for about 10–15 minutes until they are firm enough to remove using a metal spatula. Some of them will have tails of pooled, crisp praline attached to them. This is good!

12. Place the sifted icing sugar in a bowl. Gently roll each slightly warm cookie in the icing sugar. Some of it will melt. This is okay. Served warm or at room temperature, these cookies are irresistible.

Hazlenut coco clusters

YIELD: 22 COOKIES

As a chef, I love the change of seasons. Yes, summer's bounty is delicious, but when autumn arrives, a new array of possibilities presents itself. Plums and hazelnuts are two of my favorite autumn flavors. One cool, crisp Sunday morning it occurred to me that I wanted to create a recipe that would serve as a transition in my baking from summer exuberance to rustic comfort. These easy, quick hazelnut cookies are the result. If you don't have hazelnut oil, go out and get some! Make sure you store it in the fridge. Eat these with a juicy plum.

4 Tbsp	55 g	**butter**
½ cup	100 g	**sugar**
¼ cup	60 mL	**maple syrup**
1		**egg**
1 tsp	5 mL	**hazelnut oil**
½ cup + 2 Tbsp	80 g	**all-purpose flour**
2 Tbsp	30 mL	**cocoa**
¼ tsp	2 mL	**baking powder**
6 oz	170 g	**toasted, peeled hazelnuts**
7 oz	200 g	**bittersweet chocolate, chopped**

1. Preheat the oven to 350°F (180°C). Line two cookie sheets with parchment paper.

2. Beat the butter with the sugar on low speed until smooth.

3. Add the maple syrup and mix until completely smooth, about 2 minutes.

4. Add the egg, blend well, and scrape the bottom and sides of the bowl.

5. Add the hazelnut oil and mix until smooth.

6. Mix the dry ingredients together with a fork.

7. Add the dry ingredients to the butter mixture and mix on low speed until blended, about 2 minutes, scraping the bottom and sides of the bowl once or twice.

8. Crush the hazelnuts by putting them in a plastic bag and lightly banging with a rolling pin. They should be coarsely crushed.

9. Add the nuts and chocolate to the cookie batter and stir them in by hand using a rubber spatula or wooden spoon.

10. Drop by tablespoon or mini-scoop, 8 to a pan.

11. Bake for 12 minutes. Remove to a rack and cool. They will be chewy-crisp when they come out of the oven and will become crispy-chewy as they cool.

12. Store in an airtight tin for up to a week.

BROWNIE BLOBS

YIELD: 22 COOKIES

This cookie starts with the same ingredients as a brownie, measures like a brownie and looks like a brownie, but is actually a brownie blob. I just needed a break! Don't try to make the batter ahead of time or refrigerate it. Because of its high chocolate content, it'll turn rock solid in the fridge. This recipe is a great example of how milk chocolate can be successfully incorporated into a brownie without its flavor being completely overwhelmed by the other ingredients.

8 Tbsp	115 g	butter
¼ cup	30 g	cocoa
3½ oz	85 g	unsweetened chocolate
1 cup	220 g	brown sugar
3		eggs
1 Tbsp	15 mL	vanilla extract or Kahlua
3 Tbsp	45 mL	all-purpose flour
¼ tsp	1 mL	kosher salt
¼ tsp	1 mL	baking soda
1 pound	454 g	milk chocolate, chopped in chunks
9 oz	250 g	pecans or walnuts, coarsely chopped

1. Preheat the oven to 350°F (180°C). Line a cookie sheet with parchment paper.

2. In a medium saucepan over medium heat, melt the butter.

3. Whisk the cocoa into the butter. Add the bitter chocolate and whisk until melted and completely smooth.

4. Add the brown sugar and whisk until smooth.

5. Remove from the heat and let cool for 10 minutes.

6. In a small bowl, whisk the eggs until blended.

7. Add to the cooled chocolate mixture and whisk until thick and glossy.

8. Add the vanilla or Kahlua.

9. Mix together the flour, salt and baking soda. Add to the chocolate mixture and mix until smooth.

10. Using a rubber spatula, fold in the milk chocolate chunks, then the nuts. Some of the milk chocolate will melt, which is okay. It gives the cookies a nice streaky appearance.

11. Using a 3-Tbsp (45-mL) ice cream scoop or a ¼-cup (60-mL) measure, scoop out the batter, 6 cookies per baking sheet.

12. Bake for no longer than 10 minutes. Don't overbake!

13. Cool on the cookie sheet for about 5 minutes until they have firmed up slightly.

14. Remove with a metal spatula and cool on a wire rack. Store in a tightly sealed container, with parchment paper separating the layers, for up to a week.

CHOCOLATE RUGELAH

YIELD: **100** PIECES

Rugelah can be a big production, what with making the dough, rolling it, stuffing it, cutting it, and finally baking it. So make it easy on yourself and do it in stages. One day make the dough. You can freeze it for future use. Another day make the curd. The cinnamon sugar can be made at a moment's notice. Once the rugelah are formed, you can freeze them, so that when you need them you have freshly baked pastries without the fuss. Note that the technique for making the dough is similar to that of making puff pastry and creates a wonderfully flaky and multi-layered pastry.

8 oz	227 g	cream cheese at room temperature
1 cup	227 g	butter, at room temperature
½ cup	100 g	sugar
1 Tbsp	15 mL	rum or vanilla extract
2 cups	260 g	all-purpose flour
½ cup	60 g	cocoa
¾ cup	195 mL	apricot jam
½ cup	100 g	sugar
½ tsp	2 mL	ground cinnamon
4 oz	112 g	chopped toasted pecans
1 cup	125 g	dried cherries or raisins
7 oz	185 g	bittersweet chocolate, chopped
¼ cup	60 mL	melted butter

1. Place the cream cheese, butter, and sugar in the bowl of an electric mixer. Beat on medium speed until light and well blended, about 4 minutes. Mix in the rum or vanilla and beat to combine.

2. Mix the flour and cocoa together in a separate bowl.

3. Add to the cream cheese and butter and mix just until blended. The dough will be stiff and sticky.

4. Lightly flour your work surface. With a rubber spatula, scrape the dough onto the floured work surface and pat into a rectangle roughly 6 x 7 inches (15 x 18 cm).

5. Wrap in plastic and chill completely, about 2 hours or until firm.

6. Remove from the fridge and, on a surface generously dusted with flour, roll the dough into a rectangle, about 16 inches (40 cm) long and a width of about 8 inches (20 cm), with the shorter end closest to you.

7. Fold the top third of the dough down to just below the middle. Fold the bottom third over the top third. Press lightly to seal. Turn the dough 90° so the folds are perpendicular to the edge of the work surface. Flour the top and turn over. Roll and fold once again just as you did the first time.

8. Wrap the dough in plastic and refrigerate for at least an hour between each of the next turns.

9. Remove the dough from the fridge and place on the floured surface. Turn the dough so that the short end with the folds is facing you. Repeat steps 6–8 two more times, refrigerating 1 hour after each roll and fold. (You can freeze the dough wrapped in plastic and foil for a good 6 months. Defrost in the fridge before turning into rugelah.)

If the dough starts to stick to the surface, sprinkle flour on it and flip it to the other side. Brush off any excess flour. If the dough resists rolling, cover with plastic wrap and return to the fridge for about 15 minutes before resuming.

10. When ready to form the rugelah, remove the dough from the fridge and let soften at room temperature for about 15 minutes (if frozen, defrost overnight in the fridge). Cut in half. Place remaining half in fridge while you make the pastries.

11. Cover three cookie sheets with parchment paper.

12. Flour your work surface and quickly roll one piece of dough to ⅛ inch (3 mm) thick and approximately 16 inches long x 8 inches wide (40 x 20 cm). This time, the long side should be facing you. Run a metal spatula under the dough to make sure it isn't stuck to the surface.

13. Spread with ½ of the apricot jam.

14. Combine the sugar and cinnamon in a bowl, setting aside 2 Tbsp (30 mL) for Step 22. Sprinkle the dough with ½ of the remaining cinnamon sugar, ½ of the chopped nuts, ½ of the cherries and ½ of the chopped chocolate.

15. Cut the dough in half lengthwise. You will have two pieces of dough approximately 16 inches long and 4 inches wide (40 x 10 cm).

16. Holding your thumbs parallel to the dough, roll the lower half into a jelly roll about 1 inch (2.5 cm) in diameter. Don't worry if the filling starts oozing out. It always does. Turn the roll seam side down.

17. Roll the other half of the dough in the same fashion. Place seam side down parallel to the first roll.

18. Use a sharp chef's knife to cut the rolls in 1-inch (2.5-cm) pieces. Place the pieces about 1 inch (2.5 cm) apart on the cookie sheets.

19. When a sheet is full, place it in the fridge to chill the dough completely, about 30 minutes.

20. Continue rolling, filling and cutting the remaining dough. (You can chill all the cut pieces until firm and then freeze them, well wrapped, for future baking straight out of the freezer.)

21. Preheat the oven to 375°F (190°C).

22. Just before baking, brush each piece lightly with melted butter and sprinkle with reserved cinnamon sugar.

23. Bake for about 20 minutes, keeping an eye on the color (which is difficult since the dough is dark) to make sure it doesn't overbake. The dough will puff and the interior will sizzle. The rugelah are ready when the dough is firm around the edges but soft in the center.

BROWNIE POINT

Rugelah are best consumed within a day or two of baking, although they may be frozen, well wrapped, for 3 months. Reheat briefly before serving. If baking frozen, place frozen pieces on a cookie sheet and place directly into the preheated oven. Add only about 5–10 minutes to the baking time.

soft and luscious, smooth and sensual

Brownie Puddings

5

BROWNIE PUDDING

YIELD: 6 SERVINGS

I didn't grow up with chocolate pudding and never served it to my kids. Not that I had anything against it, mind you, but it just never seemed chocolatey enough. It could never triumph over a real brownie…until now. Wait 'til you try this recipe! Deep, dark, smooth as silk and rich as velvet, with a seductive, almost smoky background to the chocolate. Be careful not to burn the pudding as it cooks or you'll have more smoky flavor than anything else.

2 Tbsp	30 mL	cornstarch
½ cup	100 g	granulated sugar
½ cup	110 g	brown sugar
1 cup	250 mL	milk
1 cup	250 mL	mascarpone cheese
3 oz	85 g	unsweetened chocolate, chopped
2		egg yolks
1 tsp	5 mL	vanilla extract
1 oz	28 g	white chocolate, chopped
¾ tsp	4 mL	coffee extract (optional)

BROWNIE POINT

This pudding makes an excellent quick pie filling. Place 3 cups (750 mL) brownie or cake crumbs in the bowl of a food processor. Add ¼ cup (50 g) sugar, 2 oz (56 g) toasted pecans, ½ tsp (2 mL) salt and ½ tsp (2 mL) cinnamon. Process until you have fine crumbs. Add 2–3 Tbsp (30–45 mL) melted butter and process until the crumbs are coated. Reserve 1 cup (250 mL) of the crumbs. Press the remainder into an 8-inch (20-cm) pie pan. Bake for 10 minutes in a 325°F (165°C) oven. Cool. Pour the warm pudding into the pie shell. Decorate with the reserved crumbs by placing them around the edges of the pie. Serve with slightly sweetened whipped cream.

1. Mix the cornstarch, both sugars and milk in a medium saucepan until the dry ingredients are well moistened.

2. Add the remaining ingredients and place over low heat.

3. Stirring constantly with a wire whisk, increase the heat to medium. The chocolate will start to melt but the mixture will still be lumpy with chocolate and grainy with sugar. As it heats up, the chocolate will melt completely and it will still be fairly thin. Keep stirring, being sure to scrape around the bottom and edges of the pan where the bottom meets the sides.

4. Bring the pudding barely to a simmer. As soon as it shows signs of boiling, turn the heat down and whisk for about 1 minute or until it is thick and smooth. Remove from the heat.

5. Pour the pudding into six 4-oz (125-mL) pudding cups or wine glasses, or use a single glass bowl.

6. To prevent a skin from forming on top of the puddings, after the pudding has cooled for about 10 minutes, gently rub the tops with a piece of butter or place a piece of plastic wrap flush with the surface.

7. Serve warm or fully chilled. The pudding can last for at least 2 weeks in the fridge if properly covered and if no one digs in with a spoon!

QUICK BROWNIE PUDDING

YIELD: 6 SERVINGS

If Brownie Pudding has too many ingredients for you, try this quick version. It's more in line with traditional pudding recipes with its use of cocoa, but the addition of bittersweet chocolate will knock your socks off…and in less than 10 minutes flat, too!

¼ cup	50 g	sugar
2 Tbsp	30 mL	cornstarch
2 Tbsp	30 mL	cocoa
1 cup	250 mL	milk
3.5 oz	100 g	bittersweet chocolate, chopped
pinch		salt
½ Tbsp	7 mL	butter
½ tsp	2 mL	vanilla extract

1. Place the sugar, cornstarch, cocoa and milk in a medium-sized, heavy saucepan. Whisk to blend.

2. Add the chocolate and salt.

3. Place the pan over medium heat and bring to a boil, stirring gently but constantly as it cooks.

4. Simmer for 1 minute or until it is thickened and glossy.

5. Remove the pan from the heat and add the butter and vanilla. Stir until smooth.

6. Pour the pudding into six 4-oz (125-mL) serving cups. Serve warm or cool.

Deep, Dark Delicious chocolate mousse

YIELD: 4 SERVINGS

I stumbled upon this recipe one day as I was making Brownie Curd. I ended up whisking the cream to the point that it became whipped and voila! Quick, thick mousse. A counterpoint like vanilla whipped cream and some tart berries will round it out. Or you can just eat it out of the bowl with a spoon. Organic whipping cream is now widely available. It whips like a dream and tastes delicious!

1 cup	250 mL	**organic or regular whipping cream**
½ cup	100 g	**sugar**
½ cup	60 g	**cocoa**
pinch		**kosher salt**

1. Make sure your bowl and whisk are cold.
2. Place all the ingredients in the bowl and whisk until thickened and whipped, but not grainy.

BROWNIE POINTS

Fill baked mini tart shells with mousse for a quick, fancy dessert.

In a Champagne flute, layer whipped cream, raspberries, mousse and brownie chunks for a fabulous parfait.

Use as a filling for layer cakes.

Pipe into a rolled tuile cookie (page 112).

fudgy BROWNIe CHRistmas PUDDING

YIELD: 10–12 SERVINGS

I buy a lot of esoteric baking equipment on the assumption that one day I'll use it…which is how I came to own a classic Christmas pudding mold, a kind of deep bundt pan with a snap-on lid. The pan sat in the basement for about 10 years until I was asked to do demos for a steam oven. The pan's time had come!

1		8-oz (250-mL) jar Lyle's Golden Syrup
½ cup	60 g	cocoa
½ cup	125 mL	hot water
2 Tbsp	30 mL	instant coffee granules
1 cup	227 g	butter at room temperature
1 cup + 2 Tbsp	250 g	brown sugar
6		eggs
1 cup	130 g	all-purpose flour
½ tsp	2 mL	baking soda
5 oz	140 g	bittersweet chocolate, chopped

BROWNIe POINt

Alternatively, you can place the pudding pan on top of an empty tuna can set in a large, wide pot, such as a canning or soup pot. Add enough boiling water to come halfway up the sides of the pudding pan and seal with the lid. Cook on the stove over heat low enough to keep the water at a gentle simmer for about 1 ½ hours. Replenish the water if it becomes too low.

1. Preheat the oven to 350°F (180°C). Bring a pot of water to a simmer while you prepare the batter. Have ready a roasting pan with 4-inch (10-cm) or higher sides.

2. Grease a traditional pudding pan or 2-qt (2-L) bundt with vegetable spray.

3. Pour the golden syrup into the bottom of the prepared container.

4. Mix the cocoa, hot water and instant coffee in a small bowl until smooth. Set aside.

5. Place the butter, brown sugar and eggs in the bowl of a food processor. Pulse until smooth.

6. Add the cocoa mixture and pulse again, scraping the sides of the bowl.

7. Add the flour and baking soda and pulse just until blended.

8. Add the chocolate and pulse once or twice.

9. With a rubber spatula, scrape into the prepared pan and seal with the top if you have a steamer pan, or cover tightly with foil.

10. Set the pudding pan in the roasting pan and place in the oven. Pour boiling water ½ of the way up the sides of the pudding pan.

11. Bake in the oven for about 1–1½ hours or until the pudding is puffed. You can remove the top to check.

12. Remove the pudding pan and remove the top or foil. Place a wide plate over the top and turn upside down. The pudding will plop out surrounded by a nice, gooey sauce.

13. Enjoy while hot and serve with vanilla ice cream, sour cream or crème fraîche.

crème chocomel

YIELD: 8 SERVINGS

Is it a pudding or a custard? Who cares! It's fabulous and easy. Feel free to substitute your favorite liqueur if you don't like licorice. Raspberry, currant (cassis), orange, rum, brandy and whisky all work equally well. While you can serve the Crème Chocomel straight out of the oven, the glossy caramelized topping requires that the crème be completely chilled first, so plan accordingly.

1 ⅓ cups	325 mL	**heavy cream**
6 oz	170 g	**bittersweet chocolate, chopped**
2		**eggs**
2		**egg yolks**
1 Tbsp	15 mL	**licorice liqueur, such as Pernod**
½ cup	100 g	**sugar for caramelizing**

1. Preheat the oven to 300°F (150°C). Have ready 8 4-oz (125-mL) ramekins or custard cups, a roasting pan large enough to hold them all with space between, and simmering water.

2. Heat the cream in a small saucepan over low heat.

3. Place the chocolate in a bowl and pour the cream over top. Allow to cool, whisking occasionally. Set aside.

4. Whisk the eggs, yolks and liqueur together. Add ¼ cup (60 mL) of the chocolate mixture to the eggs. Pour the tempered egg mixture through a strainer into the chocolate mixture and whisk.

5. Pour the chocolate cream into the ramekins filling them ¾ full. Place the roasting pan in the oven and the ramekins in the roasting pan.

6. Pour enough boiling water into the roasting pan to come halfway up the sides of the ramekins.

7. Bake for about 20–25 minutes or until there is a quarter-sized area in the center of each dish that is still jiggly. Remove from the oven.

8. Remove ramekins from the water bath and let cool completely. Chill thoroughly.

9. Sprinkle each custard with a thin coating of sugar. Using a propane torch or oven broiler, caramelize the top until it is golden brown and crisp. Be careful not to let the sugar catch fire or a burned taste will permeate the pudding.

10. Serve immediately.

BROWNIE POINT

Small propane torches are now available at kitchen specialty stores. Keep the flame pointed almost straight over the sugar while waving it back and forth to avoid burning the sugar.

Plan to caramelize the puddings a few minutes before serving them. If you place the chilled, caramelized puddings back into the fridge, the sugar will eventually turn to syrup, losing its crunch completely.

yin and yang: panna cotta
and frozen hot chocolate

SERVES 4

I love contrasting something dramatically chocolate with something intensely different, like this take on an Italian pudding. Blood oranges add a tangy orange note and a fantastic pink tone to this dessert, but if you can't find them, just substitute tangerine juice.

1 cup	250 mL	buttermilk
scant ¾ cup	175 mL	mascarpone cheese
¼ cup	60 mL	blood orange or tangerine juice
1		blood orange or tangerine rind, finely grated
		pinch kosher salt
½ tsp	2 mL	vanilla extract
2 sheets		gelatin, or ⅓ envelope powdered gelatin
1 cup	250 mL	blood orange or tangerine juice
1 Tbsp	15 mL	sugar
2 cups	500 mL	Frozen Hot Chocolate (page 139), softened
2 Tbsp	30 mL	bittersweet chocolate, grated
		mint sprigs or cape gooseberries for garnish

BROWNIE POINTS

Flexible rubber baking pans in the form of mini muffins, small half-balls, or even pyramids are perfect for this recipe, since they make unmolding the custard a breeze. Pour the batter into them and chill until firm in the fridge, then place in the freezer for easy removal: just push on the bottom and out they come!

For a fancier presentation, make Tuile Cookie batter (page 112). After baking, form into a cup shape by molding the warm cookie over the top of a wine glass. Unmold the panna cotta into the tuile and scoop some Frozen Hot Chocolate next to it. Drizzle with reduced orange juice and sprinkle with grated chocolate.

1. Place the buttermilk, mascarpone, ¼ cup (60 mL) orange or tangerine juice, grated rind, salt and vanilla into a medium mixing bowl. Whisk to blend thoroughly.

2. If using gelatin leaves, soak in 1 cup (250 mL) cold water until soft, then squeeze out excess water and place in a small saucepan with ¼ cup (60 mL) cold water. If using powdered gelatin, sprinkle it over ¼ cup (60 mL) cold water in a small saucepan and let soften.

3. For both gelatins, place the saucepan over gentle heat and warm until the gelatin is completely dissolved.

4. Pour the gelatin into the buttermilk mixture and whisk to blend.

5. Pour the mixture into four 4-oz (125-mL) custard cups and chill until firm.

6. While the panna cotta is chilling, place the 1 cup (250 mL) orange or tangerine juice into a small saucepan with the sugar and bring to a gentle simmer. Cook until reduced by half. Set aside until it's time to assemble the dessert.

7. Unmold the custard cups by briefly dipping them in hot water and turning them upside down onto serving plates.

8. Place a scoop of Frozen Hot Chocolate next to the panna cotta. Drizzle the reduced orange juice around both and sprinkle both with grated chocolate. Garnish with a sprig of mint or a cape gooseberry.

9. Serve immediately.

key lime chocolate tarts (sidebar) p. 23

BUNS of CHOCOLate p. 166

JACKSON POLLOCK BARS p. 60

Holiday cookies: pâte sucrée au chocolate sandwich cookies p. 23 (sidebar)
brownie truffles with almonds, ground walnuts and sesame seeds p. 156
medjool dates stuffed with brownie curd and crème fraîche p. 140

CHOCOLate COCONUt CRème CaRameL

YIELD: 6 SERVINGS

This recipe needs to be made ahead of time and chilled if you want the full impact of the caramel oozing around the unmolded custard. If you don't care, you can eat it warm, but the caramel sticks to the inside of the cup. It's a tropical alternative to that all-time comfort food, crème caramel, and is equally pleasing, but lighter in texture and taste. It's also non-dairy.

½ cup	100 g	granulated sugar
2 Tbsp	30 mL	brown sugar
6 ½ oz	180 g	bittersweet chocolate, chopped
1 can		coconut milk, shaken well
		pinch kosher salt
2		eggs
1		egg yolk
¼ cup	25 g	sweetened coconut, toasted

1. Preheat the oven to 300°F (150°C). Have ready 6 ramekins or 4-oz (125-mL) custard cups, a kettle of simmering water and a roasting pan large enough to hold the ramekins with space between.

2. Place both sugars in a small saucepan. Add 3 Tbsp (45 mL) water. Stir briefly.

3. Bring to a boil and cover. Boil for 3 minutes.

4. Remove the cover and let the water evaporate and the sugar caramelize. If the sugar begins to brown in one area of the pan, gently swirl it to redistribute the sugar.

5. When the sugar is a deep golden brown, divide it among the ramekins. Lift each cup and swirl the sugar so it coats the bottom and some of the sides. Set aside to cool.

6. Place the chopped chocolate in a bowl. In a medium saucepan, heat the coconut milk to just below a boil.

7. Pour the coconut milk over the chopped chocolate. Let sit for about 10 minutes. Add the salt.

8. Gently whisk the coconut milk and chocolate together to make a silky smooth blend. Cool for about 10 minutes.

9. Whisk together the eggs and egg yolk. Drizzle into the chocolate mixture, whisking until smooth.

10. Pour into the ramekins, filling them ¾ full.

11. Place the ramekins in the roasting pan and the roasting pan in the oven. Pour boiling water into the roasting pan halfway up the sides of the pots.

12. Bake for 20–25 minutes or until the edges are firm but there is a quarter-sized area in the center that is still jiggly.

13. Remove from the oven and let the custards cool completely. Chill for a minimum of 3 hours or until completely set.

14. Run the tip of a knife around the edges to release the custards. Place a small plate on top and flip the cup and plate. Gently lift the cup. Sugar syrup will surround the released pudding.

15. Serve sprinkled with the toasted coconut.

pot de crème au chocolat

with variations

YIELD: 4–8 SERVINGS, DEPENDING UPON THE SIZE

Sometimes you need a dressy dessert fast, which means you don't have time for a cake, cookies or even bars. And sometimes you don't have the ingredients. Try any one of these when you're in a hurry. You'll have something rich and wonderful within 20 minutes that will satisfy and awe your diners (not to mention yourself). They're arranged in order not of complexity, but the likelihood of you having the ingredients! Because all of these recipes are so rich, I prefer to bake them in espresso cups, which offer a reasonable dessert size that's hard to resist even by the most committed dieters.

1 cup	250 mL	**whipping cream**
¼ cup	50 g	**granulated sugar**
2 ½ oz	70 g	**bittersweet chocolate chips or chopped chocolate**
4		**egg yolks**
		pinch kosher salt

1. Preheat the oven to 300°F (150°C). Have ready some simmering water and a high-sided pan large enough to hold 4 ramekins or 8 espresso cups with space between.

2. Bring the cream and sugar barely to a boil over medium heat.

3. Remove and pour over the chocolate. Let sit for about 5 minutes. Whisk until smooth. Cool for 10 minutes. You don't want the cream to cook the eggs when they are added.

4. Whisk together the egg yolks.

5. Pour the egg yolks into the chocolate mixture while whisking rapidly.

6. Add the salt. Whisk to blend. (At this point, you can store the mix in a sealed container in the fridge for up to a week. Before using, whisk until smooth. It will be thick but still pourable.)

7. Pour the mix into 4 ramekins or 8 espresso cups.

8. Place the cups in the roasting pan and add enough simmering water to the outer pan so it comes halfway up the sides of the cups.

9. Bake in the oven about 20–25 minutes or until the centers are no longer liquid but not completely firm either. They will still show some fluidity under the surface.

10. Cool for about 10 minutes before serving.

BROWNIE POINTS

This recipe lends itself to any number of flavor additions and variations. I love the contrast of the warm custards with a chilled, tangy sauce. If you choose this option, make the syrup about 2 hours ahead of the custards and chill completely.

Straining the flavored cream before mixing it with the chocolate will create a completely smooth custard, but leaving it unstrained will enhance the flavor and give varied texture. It's up to you.

meyer Lemon

Meyer lemons are sweet and tangy, smaller than normal lemons and have a thin, bright yellow skin. They can be eaten rind and all and are great added to chocolate. They are in season from late winter to early spring. You will need about 6 Meyer lemons for this recipe. Use 5 to flavor the cream and 1 for the syrup.

To make the syrup, mix ½ cup (100 g) sugar with ½ cup (125 mL) water in a small saucepan. Bring to a boil. Thinly slice 1 Meyer lemon. Drop the slices in the boiling syrup and reduce the heat to a simmer. Cook for 10 minutes. Pour the syrup into a container and chill completely.

To make the custards, follow the main recipe but add 1 Tbsp (15 mL) Meyer lemon zest to the whipping cream as it heats. Add ¼ cup (60 mL) Meyer lemon juice with the salt. Serve the custards topped with a slice of Meyer lemon in a pool of chilled syrup.

mocha

Add 1 Tbsp (15 mL) freshly ground espresso powder to the whipping cream while it heats. Add ¼ cup (60 mL) strong coffee with the kosher salt.

ginger

To make the syrup, mix 1 Tbsp (15 mL) peeled, grated, fresh ginger, ½ cup (125 mL) water and ½ cup (100 g) sugar in a small saucepan. Bring to a boil and simmer for 10 minutes. Chill. Strain before serving.

To make the custards, increase the cream by ¼ cup (60 mL). Add 2 tsp (10 mL) peeled grated ginger to the cream while it heats. Proceed with recipe as directed. When ready to serve, pour the chilled ginger syrup over each custard, and top either with finely diced candied ginger or thin slivers of peeled, fresh ginger.

pot de crème à la minute

What, another pudding recipe? After a childhood without pudding and an adulthood in search of the perfect one, I can never have enough. You won't be able to resist either.

½ cup	125 mL	half-and-half cream
1 tsp	5 mL	instant coffee granules
2 ½ oz	70 g	bittersweet chocolate, chopped
1		egg
1		egg yolk
2 Tbsp	30 mL	sugar
2 tsp	10 mL	Kahlua or brewed coffee
1 tsp	5 mL	vanilla extract
½ cup	125 mL	whipping cream
1 Tbsp	15 mL	Kahlua or instant coffee granules
		grated bittersweet chocolate or chocolate curls for garnish

1. Preheat the oven to 300°F (150°C). Have ready simmering water, 8 demitasse or 4 4-oz (125-mL) custard cups and a roasting pan.

2. Heat the cream and instant coffee in a small saucepan. Bring it to just below boiling.

3. Remove from the heat and add the chocolate. Stir gently to melt. Try not to incorporate any air bubbles. Set aside.

4. Gently whisk together the egg, yolk, sugar, the 2 tsp (10 mL) Kahlua or coffee and vanilla.

5. Pour a little chocolate cream into the egg mixture and whisk gently. Pour the remaining chocolate cream into the egg mix and stir gently to incorporate until silky and smooth. Strain into a 2-cup (500-mL) measure with spout.

6. Pour into the cups, filling them ¾ full.

7. Place the cups a few inches apart in the roasting pan. Place the pan in the oven and pour boiling water in the outer pan to come halfway up the sides of the cups.

8. Bake for 15–20 minutes or until the custard is firm around the edges but still jiggly in the center. It will continue to cook when you remove the pan from the oven.

9. Remove the cups from the water bath and let cool slightly.

10. While these are best served warm, they may be served at room temperature or chilled and served the next day.

11. Garnish with whipped cream flavored with the 1 Tbsp (15 mL) Kahlua or coffee and grated chocolate or chocolate curls (or more simply with some cold, cold cream poured on top of the hot puddings and dusted with cocoa).

BROWNIe POINtS

While you may not have half-and-half on hand, you might have vanilla ice cream. I find it is a wonderful substitute when a recipe calls for cream. I have made everything from caramel sauce to pot de crème au chocolat by substituting with vanilla ice cream. Just melt the amount you need and use it as if it were regular cream. You might want to tone down the sugar a bit, but it's not critical.

This recipe can easily be doubled or quadrupled for more servings. Just make sure the water bath allows plenty of room between the cups.

Chocolate curls are easy to make if you have a good, sharp vegetable peeler. The warmer the chocolate, the easier it is to get nice curls. You can warm chocolate the way professionals do by stroking the surface with the palm of your hand! Milk chocolate works best but bittersweet will work too. Hold the chocolate in one hand and use the peeler to strip chocolate off one of the edges. Let the curls fall onto a piece of parchment paper. Keep in a covered container away from heat.

kaffir Lime and ginger pot de crème

with chilled ginger syrup

YIELD: 8 SERVINGS

Somewhere in the 15-hour flight to visit my daughter, Joanna, in Bombay, I found myself salivating over a recipe in the *New York Times.* It explored flavors of the future and mentioned the combination of kaffir lime leaves, a staple in Thai cooking, and chocolate. I couldn't wait to try it. The result? This wonderfully subtle recipe. As predicted by the Lee brothers, the article's authors, this combination is amazing, both bold and intriguing at the same time. As usual, I've added a few chocolate touches of my own. Note that the ginger syrup must be prepared 4 hours in advance

1 cup	200 g	**sugar**
¾ cup	175 mL	**water**
1-inch knob	2.5-cm	**ginger, peeled and cut into julienne**
2 cups	500 mL	**whipping cream**
5		**Kaffir lime leaves**
1-inch knob	2.5-cm	**ginger, peeled and chopped**
6 ½ oz	182 g	**bittersweet chocolate, chopped**
1		**egg**
2		**egg yolks**
1 Tbsp	15 mL	**sugar (optional)**
¼ cup	60 mL	**double cream or crème fraîche**

1. Preheat the oven to 300°F (150°C). Have ready 8 ramekins or 4-oz (125-mL) custard or demitasse cups, a kettle of simmering water and a roasting pan large enough to hold the ramekins with space between.

2. Make the ginger syrup 4 hours or more prior to making the custards. Simmer the 1 cup (200 g) sugar, water and julienned ginger over medium heat until it has the consistency of a medium syrup, about 10 minutes.

3. Pour into a bowl, and allow to come to room temperature. Cover and chill thoroughly. About an hour before serving, place the bowl in the freezer to give it a good chill.

4. Meanwhile, assemble the pot de crème mixture. Heat the cream, Kaffir lime leaves and chopped ginger to just below a boil.

5. Place the chopped chocolate in a bowl and pour the hot cream mixture over it. Let sit for a minimum of 30 minutes, but longer is fine, too.

6. Strain the chocolate mixture into a bowl, discarding the lime leaves and ginger.

7. Whisk together the egg, egg yolks and 1 Tbsp (15 mL) sugar, if desired.

8. Gently whisk the eggs into the chocolate cream.

9. Pour the chocolate cream into ramekins, filling them ¾ full.

10. Place the roasting pan in the oven and the ramekins in the pan. Add boiling water to the roasting pan until it comes halfway up the sides of the ramekins.

11. Bake for about 20–25 minutes or until the edges are set but a quarter-sized area in the center is still jiggly. The puddings will continue to cook as they cool.

12. Remove them from the water bath and let sit for 5–10 minutes.

13. Just before serving, drop a spoonful of double cream or crème fraîche on top of each pot. Drizzle the chilled ginger syrup over all, garnishing each with shards of ginger from the syrup. Serve immediately.

BROWNIE POINTS

This recipe can be prepared up to a week in advance through step 8, making it an easy weeknight dessert when you need something deliciously special.

Kaffir lime leaves are available in most Asian and Indian grocery stores and may be frozen, stored in a plastic container, for future use.

icy, hot, fruity, fudgy

Brownie Desserts

frozen hot chocolate

YIELD: 3 CUPS (750 mL)

There's an ice cream company in my hometown that produces a wonderful zero butterfat chocolate ice "cream." One day, as I licked spoonful after spoonful from the container, I read the ingredients and decided that I could make it myself, perhaps not with its shelf-life stabilizers, but with a long enough shelf life to allow my husband and me to eat the entire batch in less than a week. I call it Frozen Hot Chocolate because it has the chocolatey richness of the drink but is bracingly cold. Don't serve it stone hard. Allow it to soften a bit or serve it right out of the ice cream freezer if you have one. And don't miss the additional Brownie Point dessert at the end of the recipe.

1 cup	200 g	sugar
½ cup	60 g	cocoa
1 ½ cups	375 mL	water
½ cup	125 mL	skim milk
½ cup	125 mL	strong, brewed coffee
1 Tbsp	15 mL	good-quality whisky (optional)
		pinch kosher salt

1. Place all the ingredients in a large saucepan.
2. Bring to a gentle simmer and stir until all the sugar is dissolved.
3. Simmer for about 15 minutes or until slightly reduced.
4. Pour into a bowl and refrigerate until cold.
5. Place in an ice cream machine and freeze according to the manufacturer's instructions, or pour into two 9- x 9-inch (23- x 23-cm) containers and store in the freezer. Every half-hour or so, use a fork to stir it up so it becomes slushy.
6. If you have frozen it solid, let it sit in the fridge for about 10 minutes or on the counter for about 5 minutes before serving to soften it enough to scoop. Or place chunks of it in the food processor and pulse until just smooth.

BROWNIE POINT

This makes a wonderfully rich smoothie. Place two scoops into a blender with a ripe banana or some ripe raspberries. Blend just enough to purée the fruit without melting the ice.

This recipe also makes easy frozen fudge pops. Pour the cooled chocolate mixutre into pop molds and freeze for about 3 hours, until firm.

medjool dates stuffed with brownie curd and crème fraîche

YIELD: 8

A few years ago, my husband, Howard, and our kids, Joanna and Alexander, drove through Napa Valley. We stopped at a gourmet store and picked up a picnic lunch, which, among other things, consisted of French prunes stuffed with foie gras. We then sat in an olive arbor overlooking a spectacular vineyard while we stuffed our faces with the most incredible prunes we'd ever eaten. This particular scene came to mind when I spotted some big, moist Medjool dates in the produce department. Having just concocted Brownie Curd, it was on my mind to do something original with it, so stuffing the curd, which has the smooth unctuousness of foie gras, into the date wasn't so far-fetched. Unlike prunes, which have a slight tartness to them, dates are really sweet, so I needed something to mediate between the richness of the date and that of the curd. I chose crème fraîche, and wow! While these can be devoured at room temperature, the flavor really shines when slightly warmed in the oven.

2 oz	56 g	**walnuts, toasted and finely chopped**
8		**Medjool dates**
3 Tbsp	45 mL	**crème fraîche**
3 Tbsp	45 mL	**Brownie Curd (page 24)**
1		**orange zest**

1. Preheat the oven to 300°F (150°C).
2. Place the ground walnuts on a plate.
3. Slice the dates open just enough to remove the pit. Do not halve.
4. Gently spread open the sides and press down the interior flesh to make some room for the fillings.
5. Using a small spoon, divide the crème fraîche among the 8 dates.
6. Do the same with the Brownie Curd, covering the crème fraîche.
7. Gently squeeze the sides of the dates towards the center to contain the filling.
8. Zest the orange over the dates so that a few strands of zest fall evenly on top.
9. Holding the dates by their sides, dip them into the ground walnuts so the top is completely covered.
10. Place the dates on a cookie sheet and warm in the oven for no more than 3–4 minutes, before the chocolate fully melts but enough to warm the crème fraîche.
11. Serve immediately.

BROWNIE POINT

Having run the Specialty Department at the Toronto Whole Foods
Market for a while, I was constantly looking for, and finding,
new cheese combinations. One of the most unusual and one
that people either loved or hated, was a Portuguese chocolate
"salami" with Gorgonzola cheese. This is definitely a variation
on the cheese course, and can substitute for dessert.

Follow the instructions, substituting crumbled Gorgonzola, or
your favorite tangy blue cheese, for the crème fraîche. Proceed
as per the recipe. What a zinger of a combination! Sweet, salty,
protein, fat and fiber…just about everything you need for a bal-
anced diet!

schrafft's nutty hot fudge/ butterscotch sundae

YIELD: 4 SERVINGS

Schrafft's restaurants no longer exist in New York City, alas. My wonderful Grandma Mae used to take me there after the movies for either a butterscotch or hot fudge sundae. To this day, I can never decide which I prefer, so I combined them and, next to a brownie, this is my favorite dessert. The key here is the temperature—the ice cream just beginning to melt on the outside so it would fall off a cone if it were on one; the hot fudge and butterscotch sauce warm and hardening as it comes into contact with the ice cream but not so hot as to liquefy the ice cream all at once. You must have a cold core. Then the nuts: lightly salted so the salt adheres but doesn't overpower the sauces. And then, of course, there's the company you devour this with. No one is allowed to mention calories, guilt or any other passion-palling topic.

8 scoops		vanilla ice cream
1 cup	250 mL	**Chocolate Fudge Sauce (page 34)**
1 cup	250 mL	**Caramel Butterscotch Sauce (page 32)**
½ cup	125 mL	**Mixed Salted Nuts (page 35)**

1. Have 4 martini glasses ready.

2. Thirty minutes prior to serving, remove the ice cream from the freezer and soften in the fridge.

3. Ten minutes prior to serving, place the Chocolate Fudge and Caramel Butterscotch sauces, if they are cold, over a pot of simmering water to soften up.

4. Pour about 2 Tbsp (30 mL) chocolate sauce in the bottom of each glass.

5. Top with a scoop of ice cream.

6. Drizzle with caramel sauce.

7. Top with a second scoop of ice cream. Drizzle with both sauces.

8. Sprinkle with nuts.

BROWNIE POINT

Coffee ice cream can also be used and is delicious.

chocolate eggnog tart

YIELD: 10–12 SERVINGS

My friend Selby recently reached into her office fridge and pulled out a container of eggnog left over from the previous weekend's Christmas party. On this particular day, I'd planned to bake a chocolate curd tart, but a light bulb went on in my head: why not make a chocolate eggnog tart instead? Here's the result. Thanks, Sel, for the inspiration.

1		**10-inch (25-cm) prebaked Pâte Sucrée au Chocolat tart shell (page 22)**
9 oz	250 g	**bittersweet chocolate, chopped**
1 oz	28 g	**unsweetened chocolate, chopped**
2 cups	500 mL	**eggnog**
2 ½ cups	625 mL	**whipping cream, divided**
2 Tbsp	30 mL	**rum**
½ tsp	2 mL	**freshly grated nutmeg**
2		**eggs**
¼ cup	30 g	**icing sugar**
2 Tbsp	30 mL	**rum**
		ground chocolate for garnish
		freshly ground nutmeg for garnish

1. Preheat the oven to 300°F (150°C). Have the tart shell ready.

2. Place both chopped chocolates in a medium-sized bowl.

3. In a medium pan, over medium heat, bring the eggnog and ½ cup (125 mL) of the cream to just below the boil.

4. Pour over the chocolate in the bowl. Let sit for 5 minutes.

5. Gently whisk the cream into the chocolate until completely mixed.

6. Add the rum and nutmeg.

7. Whisk together the eggs and gradually whisk them into the warm chocolate until thick and glossy, about 1 minute. Pour into a pitcher for easy pouring into the tart shell.

8. Place the tart shell on rack in the oven. Pour the chocolate mixture into the shell.

9. Bake for about 30 minutes or until the filling is barely set. It should still jiggle slightly in the center.

10. Whip the remaining 2 cups (500 mL) cream with the icing sugar and rum. Serve each slice with a dollop of whipped cream dusted with chocolate and nutmeg.

fresh fruit chocolate crumbles: pear, cherry, cranberry, raspberry

YIELD: 6 SERVINGS

These are the easiest and most delicious fruit desserts. You'll make them so often that soon you won't even need the recipe. In fact, I'm not going to give you one because, depending upon the fruit, you may need more or less sugar and cornstarch. Just follow my guidelines and you'll have guaranteed success. Serve warm with vanilla ice cream, crème fraîche or Crème Anglaise (page 27).

4 cups	1 L	**fruit: raspberries, cranberries, peeled and diced pears, pitted sweet or sour cherries, or any combination of these fruits**
to taste		**brown sugar (see instructions)**
to taste		**lemon or other juice, water, liqueur (see instructions)**
		cornstarch (see instructions)
		spices: cinnamon, ginger, nutmeg (see instructions)
1 recipe		**Brownie Crumble (page 38)**
		icing sugar for dusting

1. Preheat the oven to 350°F (180°C). Butter a 9-inch (23-cm) square or round glass baking dish with 2-inch (5-cm) sides.

2. Place the fruit in a bowl. Start by sprinkling with ¼ cup (50 g) sugar. Let sit for about 15 minutes. Taste the juice at the bottom of the bowl. Is it too sweet? Squeeze in some fresh lemon juice. Is it not sweet enough? Add some more sugar.

3. If your fruit hasn't given off any liquid after sitting in the sugar, add any one of the suggested liquids in the ingredient list. Cherries might not give up juice, cranberries won't, and if your pears aren't ripe, they won't either. Start with ¼ cup (60 mL) of fruit juice: orange, cranberry or even apple. Use just enough to dissolve the cornstarch. You can use liqueur, too, if you want: framboise with raspberries or Poire William with pears are fabulous.

4. Sprinkle 1 Tbsp (15 mL) cornstarch over the fruit and toss to make sure it gets thoroughly moistened by the fruit juice. Fruits that are naturally high in pectin, like cranberries, may not need this at all, but if you like your crumbles more like pie filling, then add another teaspoon or two (5–10 mL) of cornstarch dissolved in some of the liquid. Let sit for a few minutes and toss the fruit together again.

5. Add some spices to taste. Try ginger (1 tsp/5 mL) and/or nutmeg (¼ tsp/1 mL) with pears. Cinnamon is great with cranberries (1 tsp/5 mL); I don't think you need anything with raspberries but a bit of almond extract (up to 1 tsp/5 mL) is good with both kinds of cherries (try ¼ tsp/1 mL at first).

6. Tumble the entire mixture into the prepared pan, including all accumulated liquid, dissolved sugar and cornstarch and spices.

7. Top with the crumble and bake until you see the liquid bubbling around the edges and up through the center of the crumble. If it's not bubbling, the cornstarch won't thicken and you will have a grainy sauce. The crumble will be crisp and firm when done. If crumble starts to darken before the juices come to a boil, cover with aluminum foil to prevent burning.

8. Before serving, dust the top with icing sugar.

BROWNIE POINT

This is a great brunch recipe, too. The night before, prepare the berry mixture and place in baking pan. Prepare the crumble but keep it separate. Put both in the fridge. Just before baking, toss the berries to redistribute the juices. Top with crumble and bake as directed. Serve with Crème Anglaise (page 27).

CRANBERRY GANACHE CRUMBLE FLAN

(aka JOHN'S BIRTHDAY TART)

YIELD: 6–8 SERVINGS

I used to make a variation of this flan at The Original Bakery Café but we always had problems with the berries: sometimes they'd cook and sometimes they wouldn't, because we'd mound the crumble on top of them, creating insulation from the heat of the oven. Despite this, one ardent fan would purchase it for his birthday every year and even called me up at home, after the store closed, begging me to make it for him, which I did, of course, for years. When I went on to do other things, we lost touch. Imagine my amazement when he recently called me at work to order "his" tart once again. How he found me, I don't know. Here's an updated version of John's Birthday Tart. You can make this in any kind of tart shell, from 8–9 inches (20–23 cm) or even in a square or rectangular version. It's helpful if the pan has a removable bottom. You may also substitute the crumble on page 38 for the Brownie Crumble below.

CRUST:

¼ recipe	Pâte Sucrée (page 20)

1. Preheat the oven to 350°F (180°C).

2. On a lightly floured surface, roll out the pastry dough to slightly less than ¼ inch (5 mm) thick and about 12 inches (30 cm) in diameter, or at least 2 inches (5 cm) more than the size of your baking pan.

3. Fold it in half gently, lift it with your hands and place the folded side in the middle of a 9-inch (23-cm) fluted flan shell with a removable bottom. Unfold the dough.

4. Gently press the dough down into the flan shell, being sure that it fits snugly into the bottom and up the sides. Make sure there is an even amount of dough around the sides. Cut off any excess dough from the top. Prick the bottom with a fork.

5. Chill for about 30 minutes or until firm.

6. Remove from the fridge and line the pastry with foil. Fill the foil with beans or weights to help the dough hold shape while it's baking.

7. Bake for 12 minutes. Remove the foil and weights and return the flan shell to the oven. Bake for an additional 5–8 minutes, or until the shell is golden brown.

8. Remove from the oven and cool on a rack.

CRUMBLE:

3 cups	750 mL	chocolate brownie or chocolate cake crumbs
2 Tbsp	30 mL	sugar
1 tsp	1 mL	ground cinnamon
½ tsp	2 mL	kosher salt
3–4 Tbsp	45–60 mL	butter, melted

1. Mix all the ingredients together in a medium-sized bowl, adding only enough butter to create a moist but not sodden crumble.

2. Squeeze the crumbs together; some pieces should be about the size of peas.

filling and baking:

1 ½ bags		fresh or frozen cranberries, divided
¾ cup	150 g	sugar
1 Tbsp	15 mL	cornstarch
2 Tbsp	30 mL	water or raspberry liqueur
½ tsp	2 mL	ground cinnamon
⅛ tsp	0.5 mL	salt
2 cups	500 mL	Ganache (page 28)
		icing sugar for dusting

1. Preheat the oven to 350°F (180°C).

2. Place half the cranberries, and the sugar, cornstarch, water or liqueur, cinnamon and salt into a medium-sized saucepan. Stir to combine.

3. Place the pot over low heat and stir to dissolve the sugar and cornstarch. Increase the heat slightly and cook for about 5–8 minutes, stirring occasionally. As the mixture cooks, the cranberries will begin to release their juices.

4. When the filling comes to a boil, stir gently for about 3 minutes. The cornstarch will thicken the juice and it will become clear. Remove from the heat. The mixture should be lumpy with fruit in a shiny, thickened sauce.

5. Add the reserved cranberries and mix well. Cool for about 10 minutes.

6. Spread the ganache evenly over the bottom of the flan shell.

7. Give the filling one last stir before pouring it into the prepared crust. Spread evenly.

8. Distribute the crumble over the fruit.

9. Bake for 20 minutes, or until the crumble is firm and you see the filling bubbling at the edges of the flan.

10. Remove from the oven and serve warm, dusted with icing sugar and accompanied by vanilla ice cream.

BROWNIE POINT

A wonderful variation is to reduce the cranberries by ⅓ and replace them with 2 pints (300 g) of fresh raspberries, adding them in place of the second addition of cranberries.

INCREDIBLe PeaR HaZeLNUt taRt
IN CHOCOLate CRUSt

YIELD: 6 SERVINGS

Here are two great recipes in one. Pears poached in spiced red wine and served with vanilla ice cream are great in themselves. But slice the pears, place them in a crust cushioned by toasted hazelnut cream drizzled with the reduced pear poaching liquid, and you have a sophisticated and fabulous dessert. I prefer humungous red pears because you can poach them a bit longer without making them mushy, but if they're not available, any almost-ripe pear will do. Using a rectangular tart pan, as suggested, makes it easier to domino the pears, but you can just as easily use an 8-inch (20-cm) fluted round tart pan.

POACHED PeaRS

2 cups	500 mL	full-bodied red wine
½ cup	100 g	granulated sugar
2		cinnamon sticks
4		cloves
2		cardamom seeds, crushed
5		white peppercorns
2		almost-ripe pears, peeled, cored and halved

1. Place all the ingredients except the pears in a saucepan large enough to hold the whole pears submerged.
2. Bring the liquid to a low simmer and add the pears.
3. Turn the pears from time to time to make sure they are completely immersed.
4. Simmer until they are just tender at the center when pierced with a knife, about 10–15 minutes.
5. Cool the pears in the poaching liquid. If serving as poached pears, remove the pears from the liquid. Bring the poaching liquid to a boil and reduce by half. Strain. Return the pears to the liquid and reheat gently. Serve warm in bowls with crème fraîche or yogurt.

BROWNIe POINtS

The hazelnut cream in this recipe is particularly good with halved red or purple plums in place of the pears.

Toasting nuts enhances their flavor and the dish they're in, but toasting can slow you down when you are in a hurry. I like to toast a large quantity of nuts in advance and freeze them in tightly sealed, thick plastic containers. This way, any recipe can be assembled quickly.

taRt:

1 recipe		Pâte Sucrée au Chocolat (page 22)
4 oz	112 g	**whole hazelnuts, skinned**
7 Tbsp	100 g	**butter**
¾ cup + 1 Tbsp	100 g	**icing sugar**
2		**eggs**
½ tsp	2 mL	**kosher salt**

1. Preheat the oven to 350°F (180°C).

2. Roll the pâte sucrée to ¼-inch (5-mm) thickness. Press into a 14- x 4-inch (35- x 10-cm) rectangular tart pan with a removable bottom. Cover with plastic wrap and chill.

3. Place the hazelnuts in the bowl of a food processor fitted with the steel blade. Process until they are finely chopped but have not become hazelnut butter.

4. Add the butter and sugar and pulse until blended. Add the eggs and salt, pulsing until the mixture is light and fluffy.

5. Remove the tart shell from the fridge. Spread the hazelnut cream along the bottom of the crust and ¾ of the way up the sides.

6. Remove the pears from the poaching liquid (reserve the liquid). Place cut side down on a cutting board. Cut off the narrow neck portion and eat.

7. Slice each trimmed pear perpendicular to the core into ⅛-inch (3-mm) slices. Carefully slide the tip of a chef's knife under the slices and slide onto the prepared tart shell at the farthest end, overlapping the slices. Repeat with the remaining pears until the tart is neatly topped with overlapping pieces of fruit. You may not need all of them.

8. Place the pan in the oven and bake for about 40–45 minutes or until the hazelnut cream is slightly puffed but still jiggly underneath and the crust is firm. Don't overbake.

9. While the tart is baking, reduce the pear poaching liquid to ¾ cup (175 mL), or until it is thick and glossy. Be careful not to burn it.

10. Remove the tart from the oven and cool slightly before serving, drizzling each slice with the concentrated poaching liquid.

peanut butter caramel tart

YIELD: **10** SERVINGS

Oh yes, another chocolate and peanut butter recipe! I just can't help it. This is a quick and easy tart to assemble. It freezes beautifully and pleases just about everyone.

1 recipe		**Pâte Sucrée au Chocolat (page 22)**
½ cup	125 mL	**Caramel Butterscotch Sauce (page 32), cooled**
½ cup	75 g	**coarsely chopped peanuts**
½ cup	100 g	**granulated sugar**
5 Tbsp	70 mL	**peanut butter at room temperature**
5 Tbsp	70 g	**butter at room temperature**
5 Tbsp	70 g	**cream cheese at room temperature**
½ cup + 1 Tbsp	70 g	**icing sugar, sifted**
2 oz	56 g	**bittersweet chocolate, melted**
1 cup	250 mL	**Shiny Chocolate Glaze (page 19)**

1. Preheat the oven to 350°F (180°C).
2. Roll the Pâte Sucrée to a circle about 9 inches (23 cm) in diameter.
3. Press it into the bottom and sides of a 7 ½-inch (19-cm) fluted tart pan with a removable bottom. Trim any excess dough to make the top edge neat and the sides even. Wrap and freeze the scraps for another use.
4. Prick the bottom of the dough with a fork. Line with foil flush with the sides and bottom and weight with dried beans or lentils.
5. Bake for 15 minutes and remove the foil carefully. Touch the center to see if it is fully baked. If it is firm, remove from the oven. If it still feels soft and moist, bake for an additional 5 minutes.
6. Cool.
7. Spread the Caramel Sauce in the cooled chocolate shell. Place in the freezer.
8. Place the chopped peanuts on a piece of parchment paper or oiled foil. Keep them in a small circle about 4 inches (10 cm) in diameter.
9. Place the ½ cup (100 g) sugar in a small saucepan. Add 1 Tbsp (15 mL) cold water and bring to a boil.
10. Boil until the water evaporates and the sugar caramelizes into a rich golden brown.
11. Immediately pour over the nuts. Allow the praline to harden completely.

12. In the bowl of an electric mixer, beat together the peanut butter, butter and cream cheese until smooth and fluffy.

13. Add the icing sugar and continue to beat until light and fluffy. Add the melted chocolate and mix to blend, scraping the sides of the bowl. Set aside.

14. Gently warm the chocolate glaze over a pan of simmering water. It should be just warm enough to pour.

15. Remove the baked tart from the freezer. Pour ½ cup (125 mL) of the chocolate glaze over the caramel and tilt it to spread around. Work quickly because the cold caramel will set the glaze. Return to the freezer for about 5 minutes, or long enough to set the chocolate.

16. Remove from the freezer. Spread the peanut butter filling over the chocolate and smooth the top.

17. Return to the freezer for about 10 minutes.

18. Meanwhile, break the praline into small, ½-inch (1-cm) irregular pieces.

19. Warm the remaining glaze to make it pourable.

20. Remove the tart from the freezer and pour the remaining glaze over top, spreading it almost to the edges, but leaving a little filling showing.

21. Decorate around the edges with the praline pieces.

22. Serve at room temperature for best flavor and texture, but right out of the fridge with a cup of coffee is pretty amazing, too.

BROWNIE POINT

Watching those carbs but still want a great dessert? Make the peanut butter filling (steps 12 and 13). Place in plastic-lined mini muffin cups or flexible rubber baking pans with 1 ½-inch (4-cm) indentations. Spread to make smooth. Freeze completely.

Warm the chocolate glaze until it's just pourable. Pull or pop the frozen peanut butter centers out onto a rack set over a baking pan lined with parchment. Quickly pour the glaze over each serving. Place a whole peanut in the center of each dessert.

Chill for 30 minutes. Let sit at room temperature for 10 minutes before serving.

peanut butter marmalade tart

YIELD: 10 SERVINGS

If you tell your kids this is an adult version of a peanut butter and jelly sandwich, they might actually leave it all for you, or, more likely, they may discover the joys of bitter marmalade at an early age.

1 recipe		**Pâte Sucrée au Chocolat (page 22)**
1 cup	250 mL	**peanut butter**
8 oz	227 g	**cream cheese**
¼ cup	50 g	**sugar**
2 Tbsp	30 mL	**heavy cream**
2		**eggs**
12-oz jar	360-mL	**bitter orange marmalade**
1 cup	250 mL	**Shiny Chocolate Glaze (page 19)**
1 cup	120 g	**salted peanuts, chopped**

1. Preheat the oven to 350°F (180°C).

2. Roll the pâte sucrée into a 12-inch (30-cm) circle. Press into a 10-inch (28-cm) round, fluted pan with a removable bottom. Trim any excess dough, making the edges neat. Chill for at least 30 minutes.

3. Prick the bottom of the dough with a fork. Line with foil and weight with dried beans or lentils.

4. Bake for 10 minutes. If the edges are firm, gently remove the foil and continue to bake for an additional 5 minutes.

5. Remove from the oven and cool.

6. Combine the peanut butter, cream cheese, sugar, cream and eggs. Mix until completely smooth.

7. Pour into the prepared pan and bake for 20 minutes or until the filling is no longer jiggly. It will set as it cools.

8. Cool completely.

9. Warm the marmalade in a small pan and spread it gently over the cooled tart. Chill completely.

10. Barely warm the glaze over a pot of gently simmering water.

11. Pour over the center of the tart and let it spread outwards. Use a small offset spatula to quickly spread the glaze to the edges.

12. Lift the tart out of the flan ring. Place on a serving plate. Garnish all around the edges with chopped peanuts.

BROWNIE POINT

If you prefer an absolutely smooth top, rather than spread the marmalade on the surface of the baked tart, spread it in the baked shell before pouring in the filling. Proceed with baking and finishing as directed above.

BROWNIe ice cream cake

YIELD: 12 SLICES

½ recipe		any baked brownies (about 3 cups/750 mL chopped)
½ cup	85 g	peanut butter chips
3 oz	85 g	bittersweet chocolate, chopped
1 cup	250 mL	Hot 'n' Spicy Pecans (page 36)
2 pints	1 L	vanilla ice cream, softened slightly
1 cup	250 mL	Caramel Butterscotch Sauce (page 32)

1. Have a 10-inch (3-L) springform pan ready. Line the bottom with parchment paper.

2. Roughly chop the brownies into 1-inch (2.5-cm) pieces and place in a bowl with the peanut butter chips and chopped chocolate.

3. Roughly chop half the pecans and add to the bowl. Toss to mix the ingredients.

4. Scoop the ice cream into the bowl and mash in all the ingredients, using a rubber spatula. Mix thoroughly. Unless it's really hot in your kitchen, the ice cream won't melt in the less than 5 minutes that it takes to assemble this cake.

5. Scoop the mixture into the prepared pan, and spread as evenly as possible. Freeze for about 30 minutes.

6. When ready to serve, wet a kitchen towel with hot water and press against the sides of the pan. You will see the ice cream melt at the edges. Remove the sides of the springform.

7. Slide the cake onto a serving plate.

8. Drizzle with caramel sauce and sprinkle with the remaining nuts. Slice in wedges and serve each plate drizzled with caramel sauce.

banana walnut caramel crunch

chocolate pie

YIELD: 1 10-INCH (28-CM) FLAN, ABOUT 15 SLENDER BUT RICH SERVINGS

Hold the presses! I just created this for my niece Maya's seventeenth birthday and got such an incredible reaction that I had to include it in the book. Oozy, crunchy, chocolatey, it's best served warm. Chilled is fine, too, although room temperature is better. You can make it a day ahead and chill it, unglazed, then finish it with ganache shortly before serving.

¼ recipe		Pâte Sucrée (page 20)
2 Tbsp	30 mL	butter
¼ cup	55 g	brown sugar
½ tsp	2 mL	ground cinnamon
4		ripe bananas
1 cup	120 g	walnut pieces, toasted, coarsely chopped
1 cup	250 mL	Caramel Butterscotch Sauce (page 32)
1–2 Tbsp	15–30 mL	rum or water
1 ½ cups	375 mL	Ganache (page 28)
		whipped cream (optional)

1. Roll out the dough to ⅛-inch (3-mm) thickness. Press into a 10-inch (28-cm) round, fluted flan pan with a removable bottom. Trim excess dough to make the edges neat. Chill for at least 30 minutes.

2. Preheat oven to 350°F (180°C).

3. Prick the bottom of the shell with a fork. Line with foil and weight with dried beans or lentils.

4. Bake for 12 minutes until set. Remove the foil and weights and bake until golden brown.

5. Cool completely.

6. In a large sauté pan, preferably non-stick, melt the butter until bubbly.

7. Add the brown sugar and stir until the sugar and butter have turned to caramel, about 5 minutes. Add the cinnamon and blend well.

8. Slice the bananas horizontally in half. If they break into smaller pieces, don't worry.

9. Place them flat side down in the Caramel Butterscotch Sauce and sauté until golden on one side, about 3 minutes, and then gently flip them over, coating the rounded side with sauce. Cook for 1 minute longer.

10. Remove the bananas from the pan and place flat side down in the tart shell, distributing them evenly.

11. Sprinkle with half the toasted walnuts.

12. Pour the caramel sauce into the sauté pan with the banana caramel and bring to a low simmer.

13. Add the rum or water and boil for 1 minute. Remove from the heat and let cool for about 15 minutes.

14. Pour the caramel mixture over the bananas and walnuts, tilting the pan to spread it evenly.

15. Place in the fridge to cool for at least half an hour before glazing with the ganache.

16. About 30 minutes prior to serving, remove from the fridge.

17. Warm the ganache just enough for it to pour, either in the microwave on medium power or in a bowl over barely simmering water to between 80–85°F (27–30°C).

18. Pour over the caramel, tilting the pan so that the ganache covers everything. It should be even with no bumps showing.

19. Chop the remaining walnuts to a medium-fine consistency and sprinkle them either all over the top or just around the edges.

20. Serve with whipped cream.

BROWNIE truffles

YIELD: IT DEPENDS....

I watch TV while I bake, which may explain my propensity for leaving out ingredients. Who can measure accurately or at all when a crucial and sexy female character is said to possess a body part usually associated with a man (honest, "Ally McBeal," November 5, 2000)? So it was fortunate that this recipe required no measuring at all, just mixing and adding ingredients, some of which were results of my inattention. These aren't your standard truffles but they're quick and easy to make, and they make good use of leftovers and scraps.

2 cups	500 mL	**brownie or chocolate cake scraps**
½ cup	60 g	**Rummed Raisins (page 37)**
½ cup	60 g	**chopped nuts (optional)**
2–4 Tbsp	30–60 mL	**your favorite liqueur, or rum if using Rummed Raisins, or brewed coffee**
1 cup	250 mL	**Ganache (page 28)**
		cocoa for rolling

1. Place the brownie or cake scraps, raisins and nuts in the bowl of a food processor.

2. Pulse briefly to mix everything but not long enough to turn it to mush, about 3 or 4 times.

3. Add the liqueur, rum or coffee a tablespoon at a time and pulse once or twice to blend. The mixture should be barely moist enough to hold together but not mushy or wet.

4. Scrape into a bowl with a rubber spatula and refrigerate for 30 minutes.

5. Remove the mixture from the fridge and use a small scoop or teaspoon to make small balls the size of a truffle.

6. Roll between your hands to make them uniform in shape. Refrigerate for 30 minutes.

7. Barely warm the ganache. Line a baking tray with parchment paper.

8. Place a truffle on a fork and dip completely into the ganache, allowing the excess chocolate to drip through the tines and back into the bowl.

9. Use the tip of a knife to nudge the truffle off the fork and onto the parchment-lined tray. Repeat with the remaining truffles.

10. Refrigerate until the ganache is set, about 1 hour.

11. Place the cocoa in a bowl and roll each truffle in the cocoa. Place on a serving plate or in a small petit four cup for after dinner service.

12. Store in the fridge. Or freeze them and serve frozen. Amazing.

start your day the chocolate way!

Brownies for Breakfast

7

BROWNIE BRAN muffins

YIELD: 48 MINI MUFFINS, 24 LARGE MUFFINS

Everybody loves muffins. Everybody loves chocolate. Everybody loves tasty food that's healthy. So these muffins are for everybody: high in fibre, made with only whole wheat flour, they're a delicious variation on the most virtuous muffin of all. Add dried cherries, cranberries or raisins for additional flavor and fiber, or throw in some chopped, fresh bananas for a great variation. Best of all, you can make this batter and store it well-sealed in the fridge for up to a week, scooping only as many muffins as you need to bake them fresh every day.

2 cups + 1 Tbsp	240 g	brown sugar
⅔ cup less 1 Tbsp	150 mL	vegetable oil
1 Tbsp	15 mL	honey
1 ½ Tbsp	20 mL	molasses
6		eggs
¾ cup	175 mL	water
1 cup	250 mL	buttermilk
1 ¾ cups + 1 Tbsp	265 g	whole wheat flour
2 cups	150 g	bran
½ cup	60 g	cocoa
2 tsp	10 g	baking soda
½ tsp	2 mL	salt
½ tsp	2 mL	cinnamon
3 ½ oz	100 g	bittersweet chocolate, finely chopped
1 cup	250 mL	raisins, dried cherries, or diced, fresh banana (optional)

1. Preheat the oven to 375°F (190°C). Spray vegetable spray inside muffin tin or line with paper liners.

2. Whisk together the sugar, oil, honey, molasses, eggs, water and buttermilk.

3. In a large mixing bowl, mix together the flour, bran, cocoa, baking soda, salt and cinnamon.

4. Pour the wet ingredients into the dry and mix with a light hand using a rubber spatula. The batter comes together quickly and doesn't need much mixing. It will be wet.

5. Add the chocolate and any other dried fruit or chopped banana.

6. Use an ice cream scoop to portion the batter into the prepared pan.

7. Bake for a total of 20–25 minutes for large muffins, 18 for small, rotating the pan halfway through baking.

8. Great eaten warm. Store in plastic bags if not eating all at once, or freeze, individually wrapped.

BROWNIE BLINTZES

YIELD: 4 STUFFED BLINTZES

These are a real crowd pleaser. The first time I made them, I used regular blintzes, filling them with brownie batter. That was incredible enough, but I hadn't yet devised the recipe for brownie curd. So here's a chocolate upon chocolate version. If it's too rich for you, just make a normal crêpe batter and fill it with the curd instead. Either way, you may swoon! This is a small recipe. Double or triple it if you need more.

CHOCOLATE CRÊPES:

1 Tbsp	15 mL	**butter**
½ oz	14 g	**bittersweet chocolate**
½ cup	125 mL	**milk**
2		**eggs**
¼ cup + 1 tsp	55 g	**sugar**
¼ cup	35 g	**all-purpose flour**
¼ cup	35 g	**cocoa**
		pinch kosher salt

1. Melt the butter with the chocolate.

2. In the bowl of a food processor fitted with the steel blade, place the remaining ingredients along with the melted butter and chocolate and process until smooth.

3. Scrape the sides and bottom of the bowl and process briefly again.

4. Pour into a bowl and let rest at room temperature for about 15 minutes.

5. Heat up a 6-inch (15-cm) non-stick frying pan over medium heat and brush it very lightly with butter. It should be hot enough that the butter sizzles.

6. Using a ¼-cup (60-mL) measure, pour the batter into the center of the pan. Swirl into a circle covering the bottom of the pan.

7. Cook until there are bubbles on the surface of the crêpe. Use your fingers or a rubber spatula to turn it over. Cook it for no longer than 30 seconds.

8. Place on a plate and continue with the remaining batter. Stack the crêpes on top of each other to keep them moist. (They may be made ahead and frozen, with a piece of parchment paper in between each crêpe and wrapped in plastic, for up to a month. Defrost in the fridge.)

filling:

½ pint	75 g	**strawberries**
2 tsp	10 mL	**fresh lemon juice**
1 Tbsp	15 mL	**sugar**
½ cup	125 mL	**Brownie Curd (page 24)**
½ cup	125 mL	**sour cream**
		icing sugar for garnish

1. Preheat oven to 250°F (125°C). Prepare the berries: trim the stems and slice into quarters. Sprinkle with the lemon juice and sugar. Toss to coat.

2. Lay all the blintzes out on your counter. Drop 1 Tbsp (15 mL) of Brownie Curd just below the center of each one and next to it 1 Tbsp (15 mL) of sour cream.

3. Fold the bottom of the blintz up and over the filling. Fold the right hand side over the center. Fold the left hand side over the right and then roll the bottom towards the top to make a complete package. Place folded side down on a plate while you complete the rest.

4. In the same non-stick fry pan you cooked the blintzes in, melt 1 Tbsp (15 mL) butter over medium heat. As soon as the butter bubbles up and subsides, add two blintzes. Sauté until crisp and brown and place on a plate in the oven while you complete the rest.

5. Serve immediately with strawberries on the side. Sprinkle with icing sugar. Brunch may never be the same.

valentine brownie pancakes

YIELD: **16** PANCAKES

These are the perfect breakfast-in-bed treat for Valentine's Day…or any other day you want to start right with a hit of chocolate! They're decadent, fudgy and totally out of the ordinary.

1 ¼ cups	175 g	**all-purpose flour**
½ cup	110 g	**brown sugar**
½ cup	60 g	**cocoa**
½ tsp	2 mL	**baking soda**
¼ tsp	1 mL	**salt**
3		**eggs**
¾ cup	175 mL	**plain yogurt**
3 Tbsp	45 mL	**water**
2 Tbsp	30 mL	**brewed coffee**
2 Tbsp	30 mL	**vegetable oil**
1 tsp	5 mL	**vanilla extract**
1 cup	250 mL	**maple syrup**
1 Tbsp	15 mL	**Caramel Butterscotch Sauce (page 32)**
2		**medium bananas, cut into slices ⅛ inch (5 mm) thick**
¼ cup	50 g	**cinnamon sugar**
4 oz	112 g	**chopped pecans**
1 cup	250 mL	**sour cream**
		icing sugar for dusting

1. Preheat the oven to 250°F (120°C).

2. Mix together the flour, sugar, cocoa, baking soda and salt.

3. In a large bowl, whisk together the eggs, yogurt, water, coffee, oil and vanilla.

4. Add the dry ingredients and whisk gently but thoroughly. The batter will be dark and thick but it should flow off the whisk, not plop. If it plops, add an additional tablespoon (15 mL) of water. Set aside.

5. Before cooking the pancakes, pour the maple syrup into a small saucepan. Add the caramel sauce and heat gently until the caramel melts into the syrup. Keep warm over a very low heat or reheat just before serving.

6. Place a large non-stick frying pan over medium heat. Rub the bottom of the pan with butter. The butter should sizzle.

7. Use an ice cream scoop or ¼-cup (60-mL) measure to portion the batter for 3 pancakes into the pan. Immediately turn down the heat. These pancakes burn easily, so be careful to moderate your heat.

8. As soon as you see bubbles forming on top, place three slices of banana on each pancake. Sprinkle lightly with cinnamon sugar. Flip the pancakes over.

9. Continue to cook for about 2 more minutes or until the center is gently firm: it shouldn't be completely firm as they will continue to bake in the oven as you make the additional pancakes. Also, you want to maintain some fudginess, so don't overcook!

10. Remove the pancakes from the pan and place on a cookie sheet. Sprinkle with the cinnamon sugar. Place finished pancakes in the oven while you prepare the rest.

11. Cook the rest of the batter, stacking them as you go with cinnamon sugar sprinkled in between them.

12. Serve the pancakes, drizzled with the warm syrup, sprinkled with chopped pecans and dusted with icing sugar, with a dollop of cinnamon sugar-sprinkled sour cream on the side. An incredibly memorable Valentine's breakfast!

BROWNIE POINT

For a more traditional Valentine treat, omit the bananas and pecans altogether and simply serve the pancakes with fresh raspberries or strawberries in a pool of Crème Anglaise (page 27).

BROWNIE BREAD

YIELD: 1 LOAF

This bread has the flavor of chocolate with a bit of its richness, but it's definitely not a sweet bread, nor is it loaded with fat. But when I passed it around to friends at work, all true foodies, some couldn't get their heads around the idea of a chocolate bread. One even asked, "Why would anyone eat this?" Let me tell you why: toasted and slathered with Peanut Butter Brownie Curd (page 25) and topped with sliced bananas, it's the best sandwich you'll ever eat! Or spread a toasted slice with butter and sprinkle it with cinnamon sugar and you'll instantly know why anyone would eat chocolate bread! This recipe calls for a "sponge," a mixture of flour, water and yeast that helps to overcome the inhibiting qualities of cocoa on yeast. It's very easy to do and adds great flavor to the bread.

SPONGE:

2 cups	260 g	**all-purpose flour**
1 ½ Tbsp	20 mL	**instant yeast**
¾ cup + 2 Tbsp	220 mL	**tepid water**

1. In a medium-sized bowl, mix together the flour and yeast.

2. Add the water and mix to make a stiff, smooth dough.

3. Knead for about 5 minutes until there are no more lumps of flour.

4. Place in a greased bowl and cover. Place in a warm place to rise.

5. After about 40 minutes, fold the edges of the dough in towards the center. This will deflate the dough. It's okay. Cover with plastic and let double in size.

BREAD DOUGH:

¾ cup	100 g	**all-purpose flour**
½ cup	60 g	**cocoa**
¼ cup	50 g	**sugar**
2 tsp	10 mL	**kosher salt**
¼ tsp	1 mL	**ground cinnamon**
1 recipe		**Sponge**
¼ cup	60 mL	**milk**
1		**egg**
1 Tbsp	15 mL	**vegetable oil**
4 oz	112 g	**milk chocolate, coarsely chopped**
1 egg		**for glazing the bread**

1. In the bowl of a food processor, mix together the flour, cocoa, sugar, salt and cinnamon.

2. Deflate the sponge and break it up into several pieces. Place them in the bowl of the food processor.

3. Mix together the milk, egg and vegetable oil.

4. With the machine running, add the egg and oil. At first, the dough will appear streaky black and white. After about 30 seconds, it should come together into a ball. If it appears a bit dry, add up to 2 Tbsp (30 mL) water, but be restrained. Flour absorbs water over time, so it may seem like it needs moisture, when it may not.

5. As soon as the dough comes together, remove it from the processor and knead it for about 10 minutes or until it becomes smooth and slightly tacky to the touch.

6. Leave on your work surface and cover with plastic. Let it rest for 15 minutes.

7. Press the dough into a rough rectangle about 12 x 12 inches (30 x 30 cm).

8. Sprinkle ⅓ of the chocolate on the top third of the dough and fold it over towards the center, like a business letter.

9. Sprinkle the remaining ⅔ chocolate over the lower portion of dough. Fold the top half over to meet the bottom. Fold the sides in about 2 inches (5 cm) and start kneading the dough to incorporate the chocolate chunks. As you knead, the chunks may pop out. Just press them back in.

10. Shape the dough into a ball and let rest for another 15 minutes covered with plastic wrap.

11. Press the dough into a rectangle about 12 x 16 inches (30 x 40 cm).

12. Fold ⅓ down from the top and fold in 2 inches (5 cm) from each side.

13. Tightly roll the top down to meet the bottom of the dough. Pinch the edges closed to seal.

14. Place in a greased 8- x 4-inch (20- x 10-cm) pan and cover with plastic wrap.

15. Let rise in a warm place until the dough rises above the top of the pan by about 1 inch (2.5 cm). Give it time.

16. Preheat the oven to 350°F (180°C).

17. Beat the egg until frothy. Add a pinch of salt. Brush the top of the bread lightly with the egg. (You will have egg left over. Use it in another recipe.)

18. Using a sharp knife, score the bread lengthwise in a single motion.

19. Place in the oven and bake for about 30–40 minutes or until the bread sounds hollow when tapped on the bottom. I usually remove the bread from the pan after 30 minutes, tap it, and if it needs more time in the oven, let it bake further resting on its side until done, another 5–10 minutes.

20. Let the bread cool completely before slicing.

BROWNIE POINTS

Like grilled cheese sandwiches? Try sprinkling a slice of this bread with salty, grated queso fresco, a Spanish fresh milk cheese. Top with a second slice of bread. Melt some butter in a frying pan. Place the sandwich in the pan and fry until crispy on both sides.

Garnish fruit salad with thinly sliced pieces of bread, crusts removed, brushed with melted butter, sprinkled with cinnamon sugar and baked until crisp.

A wonderful variation is to add ¾ cup (75 g) of dried sour cherries or cranberries instead of, or in addition to, the chocolate chunks.

BUNS of CHOCOLate

YIELD: 12–16 BUNS

They go by various names: cinnamon buns, Chelsea buns, schnecken…and now, ladies and gentlemen: Buns of Chocolate! Big, bold, bodaciously beautiful. You will never again settle for a wimpy, white, cottony breakfast bread. This recipe looks long and complicated. Its simple subrecipes make it seem longer than it is. If you plan ahead or keep your fridge stocked with Classic Brownie batter, it can be assembled in less than half an hour.

PAN SCHMEAR:

¼ cup	60 mL	melted butter
¼ cup	60 mL	Lyles Golden Syrup or corn syrup
¾ cup	165 g	brown sugar
1 Tbsp	15 mL	rum from Rummed Raisins (page 37) or cream
1 cup	120 g	pecan pieces

1. Mix the butter, syrup, brown sugar and rum or cream until smooth.

THE BROWNIE SCHMEAR:

¾ cup	180 mL	Classic Brownie batter (page 42)
2 Tbsp	30 mL	melted butter
¼ cup	50 g	granulated sugar
½ tsp	2 mL	ground cinnamon
½ tsp	2 mL	cocoa
1 cup	175 g	chocolate chips
1 ½ oz	35 g	white chocolate chips (optional)
1 cup	250 mL	Rummed Raisins (page 37)

1. Measure out the brownie batter and butter.
2. Mix the sugar, cinnamon and cocoa together.
3. Scale the remaining ingredients and have them ready for when the bread has risen the first time.

CHOCOLATE CHALLAH DOUGH:

4 ¼ cups	550 g	**all-purpose flour**
½ cup	60 g	**cocoa, sifted**
3 Tbsp	40 g	**brown sugar**
1 Tbsp	15 mL	**instant yeast**
1 ½ tsp	7 mL	**sea salt**
1 large		**egg at room temperature**
3 ½ Tbsp	52 mL	**butter, melted and cooled slightly**
1–1 ½ cups	250–325 mL	**water**

1. Mix the flour, cocoa, brown sugar, yeast and salt in the bowl of a food processor. Pulse briefly to mix.

2. Mix the egg, melted butter and 1¼ cups (300 mL) of the water.

3. With the processor running, pour the liquid through the feed tube and process for 20 seconds. The dough should come together into a ball. When pressed, it should be soft and moist, neither wet nor dry. If it is dry and/or hard, add the remaining ¼ cup (60 mL) water, 1 Tbsp (15 mL) at a time. Let the dough rest in the bowl of the processor for 10–20 minutes to hydrate.

4. Pulse once again for about 30 seconds. The dough will be soft, tacky and a bit lumpy.

5. Remove from the processor and knead for about 5 minutes or until the dough becomes smooth. It should remain tacky but not sticky. If it is sticky, sprinkle with a little flour as you knead, being careful not to add too much. Good bread dough is always a bit tacky.

6. This is a soft dough, so it should set up fairly quickly. You know your dough is ready when it passes the so-called "windowpane" test. Remove a small ball of dough and stretch it out in opposite directions. If it breaks in two without creating a thin, almost sheer "windowpane," it is not ready. Continue to knead until it can pass the test.

7. Lightly grease a bowl with vegetable oil. Put the dough in the bowl and cover with plastic wrap.

8. After 40 minutes, it will have risen somewhat. Gently bring in the outer edges towards the center to deflate the dough. Cover and let rise until doubled in bulk, about 1 to 1½ hours.

PAN SCHMEAR:

1. Preheat the oven to 350°F (180°C). For the best-looking finish, line a 9- x 13-inch (23- x 33-cm) brownie pan with overhanging parchment paper.

2. Spread the Pan Schmear evenly on the pan bottom. Sprinkle the pecans in an even layer on top. Set aside while you roll the dough.

THE BUNS:

1. Sprinkle your work surface lightly with flour. Place the dough on the counter and press it gently into a rough rectangle.

2. Roll the dough to a thickness of about ¼ inch (5 mm). Keep lifting and flipping it over, sprinkling the rolling surface lightly with flour. If the dough resists rolling and springs back, let it rest, covered loosely with a kitchen towel, for 5–10 minutes.

3. Roll the dough into a rectangle about 8 x 16 inches (20 x 40 cm) (with the long side toward you).

4. Spread the brownie batter evenly over the dough, then brush with the melted butter. Combine the sugar, cinnamon and cocoa and sprinkle 3 Tbsp (45 mL) over the brownie batter-slathered dough. Sprinkle the chocolate chips and raisins evenly over all.

5. Starting at the side nearest you, place your thumbs under the bottom edge, and begin rolling toward the top. Every time you are about to roll up, gently pull the dough down towards you and give it a slight tug to stretch it towards you. This will extend the dough and make a tighter roll. Roll it up completely. Pinch the seam closed. Place it seam side down on the counter.

6. Place both hands over the center of the dough and gently squeeze and roll as you move your hands out to the sides. This will even out the roll, which tends to be fat in the center and thin at the ends. Don't worry if this happens. You won't notice it in the final product.

7. Use a ruler to make notches 1 inch (2.5 cm) apart. Cut the roll into 12 to 16 slices. Place each slice cut side up in the prepared pan. Don't worry if it's not symmetrical. When the dough rises, the rolls will touch each other and fill in the spaces. They will come out of the pan looking great.

8. Cover the pan with plastic wrap. At this point, you can put the buns in the fridge overnight. Allow them to sit at room temperature for at least an hour before baking the next day.

9. If you want to bake them the same day, place the covered pan in a warm place and allow to rise. This will take about 1½ hours, depending upon how warm the room is. The buns are ready to be baked when the dough keeps an indentation when gently pressed with your finger and is at least as high as the edge of the pan, if not higher by ½ inch (1 cm).

10. Preheat the oven to 350°F (180°C).

11. Place the pan in the oven and bake for 25–35 minutes. Because this is a chocolate dough, it is difficult to determine when the buns are ready. They don't "brown" like white bread dough. Trust your instincts: if you smell something wonderful, they are close to being ready. Poke the dough with your finger. If it is firm, it is ready. The centers will be softer than the edges but resist the temptation to overbake… there's nothing like warm, soft centers oozing chocolate!

12. Let the buns sit for 5 minutes before turning them upside down onto a serving platter. Turning them out of the pan while they are still warm makes sure that they come out in one piece and that all the schmear, now baked into amazing goo, follows. If there's any goo remaining in the pan, use a spatula to lift it out while it's still liquid and spread it on top of the buns.

13. These are best eaten the day they are made. But in the unlikely event that any are left over, cover with plastic wrap and reheat gently before serving the next day.

14. The unbaked, prepared buns may be frozen in the pan for future use. Cover tightly with plastic wrap and foil. Make sure the dough is completely defrosted and has risen before placing it in the oven to bake.

BROWNIE POINT

Some might think this suggestion is overdoing it, but a yummy addition to the buns is to make a simple icing sugar glaze by whisking ½ cup (60 g) icing sugar with 2 Tbsp (30 mL) milk or cream and adding some freshly grated orange zest or ¼ tsp (1 mL) of almond extract. Drizzle this all over the cinnamon buns.

chocolate french toast

YIELD: 2 SERVINGS

There's nothing like chocolate for breakfast! In the highly unlikely event that you have stale Brownie Bread (page 164), here's a great way to use it up and satisfy your chocolate craving in the a.m. It's worth it to make the Brownie Bread just so you can have it on hand for this!

⅓ cup	75 mL	whipping cream
2 Tbsp	30 mL	milk or skim milk
2		eggs
1 Tbsp	15 mL	sugar
1 tsp	5 mL	vanilla extract
1 tsp	5 mL	rum
		pinch kosher salt
4 pieces		stale Brownie Bread, sliced ½ inch (1 cm) thick
4 Tbsp	55 g	butter
¼ cup	50 g	sugar
¼ tsp	1 mL	cinnamon
2 Tbsp	30 mL	crème fraîche
1 pint	150 g	fresh raspberries

1. Preheat the oven to 250°F (120°C).

2. Whisk the cream, milk, eggs, sugar, vanilla, rum and salt in a wide bowl.

3. Place one piece of bread in the mixture. Allow the bread to become saturated but not so soft that it will fall apart when lifted.

4. Meanwhile, heat 1 Tbsp (15 mL) butter until frothy in a medium-sized, non-stick frying pan over medium heat.

5. Add the soaked bread and cook until crisp on one side. Add more butter before turning to cook the other side. While you are cooking the first piece, place the second piece in the soaking mixture.

6. Place the cooked french toast on a baking sheet in the oven while you prepare the remaining pieces.

7. Remove from the oven and place on two plates. Mix the sugar with the cinnamon and sprinkle on top. Garnish with crème fraîche and fresh berries.

stuffed brownie french toast for two

If the above recipe isn't decadent enough for you, here's another. Lay 4 slices of stale Brownie Bread (page 164) on the counter. Spread two with cream cheese, the other two with a generous layer of Brownie Curd (page 24). If you're really ravenous, top one side with one or two of the following: sliced bananas, fresh berries, chopped nuts. Sandwich a cream cheese slice with a Brownie Curd slice and proceed with dipping and frying as above. Slice in half and serve with the cut side showing. Dust with icing sugar and serve with maple syrup.

INDEX